# KNOW YOUR GOVERNMENT

# The Federal Government: How It Works

KNOW YOUR GOVERNMENT

# The Federal Government: How It Works

Bob Bernotas

CHELSEA HOUSE PUBLISHERS

On the cover: *Left:* A voter casts his ballot. *Top right:* The Capitol. *Middle right:* The U.S. Supreme Court Building. *Bottom right:* The White House.
Frontispiece: The Capitol.

**Chelsea House Publishers**
Editor-in-Chief: Nancy Toff
Executive Editor: Remmel T. Nunn
Managing Editor: Karyn Gullen Browne
Copy Chief: Juliann Barbato
Picture Editor: Adrian G. Allen
Art Director: Maria Epes
Manufacturing Manager: Gerald Levine

**Know Your Government**
Senior Editor: Kathy Kuhtz

**Staff for THE FEDERAL GOVERNMENT: HOW IT WORKS**
Associate Editor: Scott Prentzas
Copy Editor: Brian Sookram
Deputy Copy Chief: Mark Rifkin
Picture Researcher: Merlinda Fournier
Picture Coordinator: Melanie Sanford
Assistant Art Director: Loraine Machlin
Senior Designer: Noreen M. Lamb
Production Manager: Joseph Romano
Production Coordinator: Marie Claire Cebrián

**Library of Congress Cataloging-in-Publication Data**

Bernotas, Bob.
   The Federal government: how it works / Bob Bernotas.
      p.   cm.—(Know your government)
   Includes bibliographical references.
   Summary: Surveys the history of the federal government and describes its structure and current functions.
   ISBN 0-87754-859-5
        0-7910-0895-9 (pbk.)
   1. United States—Politics and government—Juvenile literature.   [1. United States—Politics and government.   I. Title.   II. Series: Know your government (New York, N.Y.)
JK40.B47   1990                                                                        89-49223
320.473—dc20                                                                              CIP
                                                                                          AC

# CONTENTS

# KNOW YOUR GOVERNMENT

CHELSEA HOUSE PUBLISHERS

# INTRODUCTION

# Government: Crises of Confidence

## Arthur M. Schlesinger, jr.

From the start, Americans have regarded their government with a mixture of reliance and mistrust. The men who founded the republic did not doubt the indispensability of government. "If men were angels," observed the 51st Federalist Paper, "no government would be necessary." But men are not angels. Because human beings are subject to wicked as well as to noble impulses, government was deemed essential to assure freedom and order.

At the same time, the American revolutionaries knew that government could also become a source of injury and oppression. The men who gathered in Philadelphia in 1787 to write the Constitution therefore had two purposes in mind. They wanted to establish a strong central authority and to limit that central authority's capacity to abuse its power.

To prevent the abuse of power, the Founding Fathers wrote two basic principles into the new Constitution. The principle of federalism divided power between the state governments and the central authority. The principle of the separation of powers subdivided the central authority itself into three branches—the executive, the legislative, and the judiciary—so that "each may be a check on the other." The *Know Your Government* series focuses on the major executive departments and agencies in these branches of the federal government.

7

The Constitution did not plan the executive branch in any detail. After vesting the executive power in the president, it assumed the existence of "executive departments" without specifying what these departments should be. Congress began defining their functions in 1789 by creating the Departments of State, Treasury, and War. The secretaries in charge of these departments made up President Washington's first cabinet. Congress also provided for a legal officer, and President Washington soon invited the attorney general, as he was called, to attend cabinet meetings. As need required, Congress created more executive departments.

Setting up the cabinet was only the first step in organizing the American state. With almost no guidance from the Constitution, President Washington, seconded by Alexander Hamilton, his brilliant secretary of the treasury, equipped the infant republic with a working administrative structure. The Federalists believed in both executive energy and executive accountability and set high standards for public appointments. The Jeffersonian opposition had less faith in strong government and preferred local government to the central authority. But when Jefferson himself became president in 1801, although he set out to change the direction of policy, he found no reason to alter the framework the Federalists had erected.

By 1801 there were about 3,000 federal civilian employees in a nation of a little more than 5 million people. Growth in territory and population steadily enlarged national responsibilities. Thirty years later, when Jackson was president, there were more than 11,000 government workers in a nation of 13 million. The federal establishment was increasing at a faster rate than the population.

Jackson's presidency brought significant changes in the federal service. He believed that the executive branch contained too many officials who saw their jobs as "species of property" and as "a means of promoting individual interest." Against the idea of a permanent service based on life tenure, Jackson argued for the periodic redistribution of federal offices, contending that this was the democratic way and that official duties could be made "so plain and simple that men of intelligence may readily qualify themselves for their performance." He called this policy rotation-in-office. His opponents called it the spoils system.

In fact, partisan legend exaggerated the extent of Jackson's removals. More than 80 percent of federal officeholders retained their jobs. Jackson discharged no larger a proportion of government workers than Jefferson had done a generation earlier. But the rise in these years of mass political parties gave federal patronage new importance as a means of building the party and of rewarding activists. Jackson's successors were less restrained in the distribu-

8

tion of spoils. As the federal establishment grew—to nearly 40,000 by 1861—the politicization of the public service excited increasing concern.

After the Civil War the spoils system became a major political issue. High-minded men condemned it as the root of all political evil. The spoilsmen, said the British commentator James Bryce, "have distorted and depraved the mechanism of politics." Patronage, by giving jobs to unqualified, incompetent, and dishonest persons, lowered the standards of public service and nourished corrupt political machines. Office-seekers pursued presidents and cabinet secretaries without mercy. "Patronage," said Ulysses S. Grant after his presidency, "is the bane of the presidential office." "Every time I appoint someone to office," said another political leader, "I make a hundred enemies and one ingrate." George William Curtis, the president of the National Civil Service Reform League, summed up the indictment. He said,

> The theory which perverts public trusts into party spoils, making public
> employment dependent upon personal favor and not on proved merit,
> necessarily ruins the self-respect of public employees, destroys the
> function of party in a republic, prostitutes elections into a desperate
> strife for personal profit, and degrades the national character by lower-
> ing the moral tone and standard of the country.

The object of civil service reform was to promote efficiency and honesty in the public service and to bring about the ethical regeneration of public life. Over bitter opposition from politicians, the reformers in 1883 passed the Pendleton Act, establishing a bipartisan Civil Service Commission, competitive examinations, and appointment on merit. The Pendleton Act also gave the president authority to extend by executive order the number of "classified" jobs—that is, jobs subject to the merit system. The act applied initially only to about 14,000 of the more than 100,000 federal positions. But by the end of the 19th century 40 percent of federal jobs had moved into the classified category.

Civil service reform was in part a response to the growing complexity of American life. As society grew more organized and problems more technical, official duties were no longer so plain and simple that any person of intelligence could perform them. In public service, as in other areas, the all-round man was yielding ground to the expert, the amateur to the professional. The excesses of the spoils system thus provoked the counter-ideal of scientific public administration, separate from politics and, as far as possible, insulated against it.

The cult of the expert, however, had its own excesses. The idea that administration could be divorced from policy was an illusion. And in the realm of policy, the expert, however much segregated from partisan politics, can never attain perfect objectivity. He remains the prisoner of his own set of values. It is these values rather than technical expertise that determine fundamental judgments of public policy. To turn over such judgments to experts, moreover, would be to abandon democracy itself; for in a democracy final decisions must be made by the people and their elected representatives. "The business of the expert," the British political scientist Harold Laski rightly said, "is to be on tap and not on top."

Politics, however, were deeply ingrained in American folkways. This meant intermittent tension between the presidential government, elected every four years by the people, and the permanent government, which saw presidents come and go while it went on forever. Sometimes the permanent government knew better than its political masters; sometimes it opposed or sabotaged valuable new initiatives. In the end a strong president with effective cabinet secretaries could make the permanent government responsive to presidential purpose, but it was often an exasperating struggle.

The struggle within the executive branch was less important, however, than the growing impatience with bureaucracy in society as a whole. The 20th century saw a considerable expansion of the federal establishment. The Great Depression and the New Deal led the national government to take on a variety of new responsibilities. The New Deal extended the federal regulatory apparatus. By 1940, in a nation of 130 million people, the number of federal workers for the first time passed the 1 million mark. The Second World War brought federal civilian employment to 3.8 million in 1945. With peace, the federal establishment declined to around 2 million by 1950. Then growth resumed, reaching 2.8 million by the 1980s.

The New Deal years saw rising criticism of "big government" and "bureaucracy." Businessmen resented federal regulation. Conservatives worried about the impact of paternalistic government on individual self-reliance, on community responsibility, and on economic and personal freedom. The nation in effect renewed the old debate between Hamilton and Jefferson in the early republic, although with an ironic exchange of positions. For the Hamiltonian constituency, the "rich and well-born," once the advocate of affirmative government, now condemned government intervention, while the Jeffersonian constituency, the plain people, once the advocate of a weak central government and of states' rights, now favored government intervention.

In the 1980s, with the presidency of Ronald Reagan, the debate has burst out with unusual intensity. According to conservatives, government intervention abridges liberty, stifles enterprise, and is inefficient, wasteful, and

10

arbitrary. It disturbs the harmony of the self-adjusting market and creates worse troubles than it solves. Get government off our backs, according to the popular cliché, and our problems will solve themselves. When government is necessary, let it be at the local level, close to the people. Above all, stop the inexorable growth of the federal government.

In fact, for all the talk about the "swollen" and "bloated" bureaucracy, the federal establishment has not been growing as inexorably as many Americans seem to believe. In 1949, it consisted of 2.1 million people. Thirty years later, while the country had grown by 70 million, the federal force had grown only by 750,000. Federal workers were a smaller percentage of the population in 1985 than they were in 1955—or in 1940. The federal establishment, in short, has not kept pace with population growth. Moreover, national defense and the postal service account for 60 percent of federal employment.

Why then the widespread idea about the remorseless growth of government? It is partly because in the 1960s the national government assumed new and intrusive functions: affirmative action in civil rights, environmental protection, safety and health in the workplace, community organization, legal aid to the poor. Although this enlargement of the federal regulatory role was accompanied by marked growth in the size of government on all levels, the expansion has taken place primarily in state and local government. Whereas the federal force increased by only 27 percent in the 30 years after 1950, the state and local government force increased by an astonishing 212 percent.

Despite the statistics, the conviction flourishes in some minds that the national government is a steadily growing behemoth swallowing up the liberties of the people. The foes of Washington prefer local government, feeling it is closer to the people and therefore allegedly more responsive to popular needs. Obviously there is a great deal to be said for settling local questions locally. But local government is characteristically the government of the locally powerful. Historically, the way the locally powerless have won their human and constitutional rights has often been through appeal to the national government. The national government has vindicated racial justice against local bigotry, defended the Bill of Rights against local vigilantism, and protected natural resources against local greed. It has civilized industry and secured the rights of labor organizations. Had the states' rights creed prevailed, there would perhaps still be slavery in the United States.

The national authority, far from diminishing the individual, has given most Americans more personal dignity and liberty than ever before. The individual freedoms destroyed by the increase in national authority have been in the main

11

the freedom to deny black Americans their rights as citizens; the freedom to put small children to work in mills and immigrants in sweatshops; the freedom to pay starvation wages, require barbarous working hours, and permit squalid working conditions; the freedom to deceive in the sale of goods and securities; the freedom to pollute the environment—all freedoms that, one supposes, a civilized nation can readily do without.

"Statements are made," said President John F. Kennedy in 1963, "labelling the Federal Government an outsider, an intruder, an adversary. . . . The United States Government is not a stranger or not an enemy. It is the people of fifty states joining in a national effort. . . . Only a great national effort by a great people working together can explore the mysteries of space, harvest the products at the bottom of the ocean, and mobilize the human, natural, and material resources of our lands."

So an old debate continues. However, Americans are of two minds. When pollsters ask large, spacious questions—Do you think government has become too involved in your lives? Do you think government should stop regulating business?—a sizable majority opposes big government. But when asked specific questions about the practical work of government—Do you favor social security? unemployment compensation? Medicare? health and safety standards in factories? environmental protection? government guarantee of jobs for everyone seeking employment? price and wage controls when inflation threatens?—a sizable majority approves of intervention.

In general, Americans do not want less government. What they want is more efficient government. They want government to do a better job. For a time in the 1970s, with Vietnam and Watergate, Americans lost confidence in the national government. In 1964, more than three-quarters of those polled had thought the national government could be trusted to do right most of the time. By 1980 only one-quarter was prepared to offer such trust. But by 1984 trust in the federal government to manage national affairs had climbed back to 45 percent.

Bureaucracy is a term of abuse. But it is impossible to run any large organization, whether public or private, without a bureaucracy's division of labor and hierarchy of authority. And we live in a world of large organizations. Without bureaucracy modern society would collapse. The problem is not to abolish bureaucracy, but to make it flexible, efficient, and capable of innovation.

Two hundred years after the drafting of the Constitution, Americans still regard government with a mixture of reliance and mistrust—a good combination. Mistrust is the best way to keep government reliable. Informed criticism

12

is the means of correcting governmental inefficiency, incompetence, and arbitrariness; that is, of best enabling government to play its essential role. For without government, we cannot attain the goals of the Founding Fathers. Without an understanding of government, we cannot have the informed criticism that makes government do the job right. It is the duty of every American citizen to know our government—which is what this series is all about.

*The delegates to the Constitutional Convention sign the Constitution on September 17, 1787. The Constitution of the United States delineated the structure and powers of a new national government that has evolved and expanded greatly over the past 200 years.*

# ONE

# The Federal Government and the Constitution

*Fed Dems*

In the late spring of 1787, 55 delegates from the 13 newly independent American states met in Philadelphia to establish the structure and powers of a new national government. Over the course of the next two centuries, that government would evolve, adapting to changes, great and small, in American society and the world. Yet the basic framework of the federal government has changed very little. This combination of flexibility and stability stands as a testimony to the care and foresight with which men such as James Madison, Alexander Hamilton, and Benjamin Franklin crafted the document known as the Constitution of the United States.

The Constitution was not born out of theory and reflection alone. It was also a necessary and practical response to serious problems facing the new nation. When the British surrender at Yorktown in October 1781 ended the revolutionary war, the 13 former colonies constituted themselves into a loose league of friendship under a framework called the Articles of Confederation. The confederation, however, soon proved to be a weak and impractical structure, a poor substitute for a true national government. Under the Articles of Confederation, the Continental Congress did not have the power to levy taxes.

No national court system existed. There was no president. The articles could be amended only with the unanimous consent of the 13 states. Because conflicting interests nearly always kept the states at odds, amendments would have been virtually impossible to obtain in practice. In short, the first American government, under the articles, could neither enforce nor increase its limited powers.

Soon, serious quarrels broke out among states over boundaries and taxes on imported goods, known as tariffs, threatening what little unity there was. Then, in 1786 a major economic depression left many farmers in debt, hungry, and angry. The upper classes feared the possibility of a revolution by the poor. Finally, James Madison of Virginia and Alexander Hamilton of New York were able to convince the states to call a convention to be held in Philadelphia in May 1787 for the purpose of reconstituting the national government.

Near the end of 1786, a group of Massachusetts farmers, unable to pay their mortgages and taxes, tried to prevent the courts from foreclosing the mortgages on their farms. Led by Daniel Shays, they marched on the Springfield arsenal to get weapons but were defeated by the state militia. Nevertheless, their act, remembered as Shays's Rebellion, raised the specter of "mob rule" and helped shift public opinion in favor of a new, strong, and stable federal government.

# The Powers of the Federal Government

In June 1788, the Constitution went into effect, having been ratified, or approved, by 9 of the 13 states. It was almost two years later, in May 1790, that the last state, Rhode Island, ratified the Constitution and joined the union. By then, George Washington had been president for more than a year.

The Constitution defined the powers of the federal government. It also left open broad areas that were filled in, over time, by the actions of various presidents and Congresses and the rulings of the Supreme Court. There are four general types of federal powers: enumerated, concurrent, inherent, and implied.

In such phrases as, "The Congress shall have Power To lay and collect Taxes, Duties, Imposts, and Excises" (Article I, Section 8) and "The President shall be Commander in Chief of the Army and Navy of the United States" (Article II, Section 2), the framers of the Constitution set out the federal government's *enumerated powers*. These are, simply, the specific powers that are granted to the government by the Constitution.

16

Some federal powers, such as the power to tax, are held by both the federal government and the various state governments. These are called *concurrent powers* because they are exercised independently by different levels of government. Of course, many federal powers are not held concurrently by the states, for example, the power to coin money or to declare war on a foreign country.

Certain federal powers, according to Supreme Court decisions, need not be enumerated in the Constitution to be exercised. They are *inherent powers* that are necessary and basic to the functioning of any national government. For example, in a world of separate and often conflicting nations, the U.S. government must be able to deal with other countries. Thus, the federal government, said the Supreme Court, would have the power to conduct relations with foreign nations even if it were not mentioned in the Constitution.

Finally, there are *implied powers* that are not spelled out in the Constitution, but nevertheless, as the Supreme Court has ruled, may be exercised by the federal government. The framers of that document understood that in order to deal with new political problems and changing social conditions in years to come, the government would have to expand its existing powers or take on additional ones. For example, who would have expected in 1787 that some day Congress would be compelled to create a National Aeronautics and Space Administration (NASA) to promote the exploration of outer space? These implied powers are derived from the last paragraph of Article I, Section 8, known as the "elastic clause," which gives Congress the power "to make all Laws which shall be necessary and proper" to carry out the functions of government set down elsewhere in the Constitution. Although the elastic clause was included in the original document of 1787, it took more than 30 years for the concept of implied powers to be established in practice.

In 1819, the Supreme Court, under the leadership of Chief Justice John Marshall, unanimously ruled in the case of *McCulloch v. Maryland* that the creation of a national bank was a "necessary and proper" way for Congress to exercise its constitutionally enumerated powers to collect taxes, borrow money, and regulate commerce. Marshall argued that all acts of the government that are not prohibited by the Constitution are legitimate and lawful. In other words, the Constitution did not have to state exactly all the things that the federal government may do. It need only say what the government cannot do. The Court's landmark decision in *McCulloch* made possible a broad expansion of federal power, which was most evident a century later when the federal government confronted the social changes and problems typical of a rapidly industrialized and urbanized society such as poverty, unemployment,

17

*During Chief Justice John Marshall's term (1801–35), the Supreme Court strengthened the powers of the federal government by ruling that it could legitimately exercise authority over all matters except those prohibited by the Constitution.*

housing shortages, labor-management conflicts, resource use, and economic fluctuations. Since the mid-1930s, virtually all of the important acts of the federal government have been derived from the concept of implied powers as laid down in the elastic clause and established by the Supreme Court in *McCulloch*.

# The Branches of Government

Article I of the Constitution gives "all legislative Powers," that is, the power to make all the laws, to Congress. It establishes a bicameral (two-house) legislature made up of the Senate and the House of Representatives. Article I also spells out the age and citizenship requirements, length of terms, powers, duties, and, to some extent, structures and procedures for each house of Congress.

According to Article II, "the executive Power," the power to carry out the laws that Congress makes, is vested in "a President of the United States of America." Article II also sets down the eligibility requirements for the office and explains how the president and vice-president are elected. Finally, it gives the president authority over the armed forces and the power to make treaties and to appoint ambassadors, judges, and other high government officials.

In Article III, "the judicial Power" is vested in "one supreme Court, and in such inferior Courts" as Congress may create. The article states that the jurisdiction of these courts "shall extend . . . to all Cases arising under this Constitution, the Laws of the United States, and Treaties made . . . under their Authority." Thus, the Supreme Court has the power to review all acts of Congress and decide whether they violate the Constitution.

The federal government, therefore, is composed of three branches— legislative, executive, and judicial. This principle of *separation of powers* originated with the French political philosopher Baron de Montesquieu, who believed that the best way to protect liberty was to divide the functions of government among distinct branches. The authors of the Constitution were influenced by Montesquieu's idea and incorporated it into their notion of three equal and independent branches of government.

To reinforce this separation of powers, the Constitution created a different way of selecting the officials of each of the three branches. Members of the House of Representatives are elected by "the people," which, at the time, meant white males who, in general, owned property. Senators originally were chosen by the state legislatures. (The Seventeenth Amendment, ratified in

*In 1748, the French political philosopher Baron de Montesquieu wrote* The Spirit of Laws. *Montesquieu's treatise greatly influenced the framers of the U.S. Constitution, who adopted his theory that a government's powers should be divided among equal and independent branches.*

1913, established direct election of senators by the voters.) The president is chosen by the electoral college system, in which electors from each of the 50 states formally elect the president and vice-president. In the view of many contemporary observers, however, the electoral college system is complicated and outdated and should be replaced by direct election by the voters. Finally, federal judges are appointed by the president "with the Advice and Consent of the Senate."

The terms of office also vary among the three branches. Representatives serve a two-year term, and all face reelection at the same time. Senators serve a six-year term, with one-third of them running for reelection every two years. The president holds office for a four-year term. Federal judges, the Constitution states, "shall hold their offices during good Behaviour," which essentially amounts to lifetime tenure.

Along with separating the powers of the federal government, the Constitution also created a system of *checks and balances*. These provisions allow one branch to control, or check, the power of the other two, so that no single branch can become too powerful, at least in theory. For example, the president may veto laws passed by Congress, which, in turn, can override the president's veto with a two-thirds majority in both houses. The president is commander in chief of the armed forces, but only Congress has the power to declare war. Presidential appointments to positions in both the executive and judicial branches are subject to approval by the Senate, which sometimes rejects presidential nominees. The Supreme Court can rule that laws made by Congress or actions of the president are unconstitutional. Even so, over time the executive has emerged as the most powerful branch in the areas of foreign and domestic policy. However, without the system of checks and balances, the executive branch might have grown arbitrary and tyrannical in its exercise of power.

Therefore, the doctrine of separation of powers gives each branch of the federal government its own realm of authority, whereas the system of checks and balances allows intrusions upon that authority by the other branches. Because of this constitutional paradox, the powers and responsibilities of the branches tend to overlap in practice. Congress makes laws; the president has veto power over those laws; and the Supreme Court ultimately decides whether the laws are legitimate. Moreover, the president frequently initiates legislation through the sponsorship of loyal party members in Congress. And Supreme Court rulings, such as its decision in *Brown v. Board of Education of Topeka, Kansas* (1954) that outlawed segregation in public schools, clearly have the impact of law. In this way, each branch exercises the legislative power

*On the steps of the U.S. Supreme Court, Nettie Hunt explains to her daughter the Court's decision in* Brown v. Board of Education of Topeka, Kansas *(1954), which outlawed segregation in public schools. Supreme Court rulings play a major role in the development of government policy by applying the Constitution to social and political issues that the executive and legislative branches have failed to confront.*

that, according to Article I, was vested in Congress alone. In addition, the realities of the 20th-century world have helped to erode the notion of distinct realms of governmental authority. For example, faced with an imminent nuclear attack, a president would not have the time to wait while Congress debates and then votes on a formal declaration of war.

In short, the government of the United States is a government of shared powers, which tends to create a certain tension among the branches. The framers of the Constitution wanted a balanced government in which none of the single components could gain enough power to dominate the others. Each part would have to compromise in order to create policies that are in the common interest. In a very real way, then, politics at the federal level involves the resolution of built-in tensions and conflicts so that policies can be made effectively and carried out efficiently.

# The Purpose of This Book

The following chapters examine more closely the individual parts of the federal government: Congress, the presidency, the federal judiciary, and—what many political observers consider to be the fourth branch of the government—the federal bureaucracy. The particular structure of each component will be discussed and its functions and procedures outlined in order to develop a clearer understanding of the inner workings and interactions of these separate, but overlapping, branches.

In addition to these formal institutions, it is necessary to examine some of the powerful external forces—interest groups, lobbyists, and political action committees (PACs)—that influence the actions and policies of the federal government. Finally, because the government in Washington, D.C., sits atop a multilevel governmental structure, it is important to consider how it interacts with the many state and local units of government that compose the American federalist system.

Overall, then, this book is concerned with the mechanics of government in the United States, literally "how it works," in theory and, even more importantly, in practice.

*Speaker of the House Thomas P. "Tip" O'Neill administers the oath of office to members of the House of Representatives as the 97th Congress convenes in January 1981. The House of Representatives and the Senate constitute the legislative branch of the federal government.*

# TWO

# Congress

The legislative branch of the federal government, known as Congress, is bicameral, that is, it consists of two chambers, the Senate and the House of Representatives. Although both of these houses are responsible for making the laws that govern the nation, they are quite different in terms of their structures, rules, traditions, and character.

## The House of Representatives

The House of Representatives is made up of 435 members from the 50 states. According to the Constitution, to be elected to the House, a person must be at least 25 years of age, a citizen for at least 7 years, and an inhabitant of the state from which he or she is elected. For the purpose of choosing members of the House of Representatives, each state is divided into separate congressional districts from which a representative is elected. Every two years the entire House must run for reelection.

The number of representatives from each state is proportional to its population. The more populous states, such as California and New York, have more representatives, and the less populous, such as Montana and Alaska, have fewer. Periodically, as the population of the United States shifts, states lose or gain representatives. The most powerful member of the House of

# Congress and Ethics: The Resignation of Jim Wright, Speaker of the House

Almost from the day in 1987 when he succeeded Thomas P. "Tip" O'Neill as Speaker of the House, Texas Democrat Jim Wright was immersed in controversy, much of it the result of his political style. Throughout the Reagan years, the congenial O'Neill played the role of the loyal opposition. Wright, however, was pugnacious and abrasive, and he attempted to run the House in an uncompromisingly partisan manner. As Speaker, Tip O'Neill had political opponents; Jim Wright, on the other hand, made political enemies.

In 1988, Wright's enemies in the Republican party attacked him over a lucrative book deal with a political supporter, an arrangement that looked suspiciously like an under-the-table campaign contribution. Also questioned were gifts that Wright and his wife, Betty, received from a failing Texas savings and loan institution. During this time, the House was drafting legislation to bail out savings and loans. These apparent violations of campaign law and the conflict of interest led to an investigation by the House Ethics Committee and calls by House Republicans for Wright's removal.

The House can exercise a range of actions against a member who is charged with ethical wrongdoing. The ethics committee, after completing its investigation, can issue a letter of rebuke, which would end the matter. The panel could recommend to the full House that the member be reprimanded, in effect a slap on the wrist, or censured, a more serious step. If the member is part of the House leadership, he or she can be removed from that position. Finally, the House can vote to expel a member.

In the 200-year history of the House, only 4 members have been expelled. The House has censured 23 members. A Speaker of the House has never been censured or expelled, although in 1910, Speaker Joseph G. Cannon, who since 1903 had ruled the body zealously and autocratically, was stripped of much of his power, and the next year he was defeated as Speaker.

Wright's case, however, never reached that point. After a lengthy investigation, the ethics committee charged him with 69 violations of House ethics rules. On May 31, 1989, Wright, rather than defend himself formally against these charges and face possible punitive action, resigned both his post as Speaker and the House seat that he had held for 35 years. House Democrats selected majority leader Thomas Foley of Washington as the new Speaker.

In the midst of the Wright affair, House majority whip Tony Coelho of California, an up-and-coming Democrat, resigned after reports of questionable financial practices. A number of other House members faced either legal charges or ethics investigations. Notably, minority whip Newt Gingrich of Georgia, Wright's chief accuser, was said to have benefited improperly from his own book promotion deal. Some House members were charged with sexual misconduct.

At the end of 1989, the Senate Ethics Committee began a preliminary investigation of seven senators. Six were accused of intervening improperly with federal savings and loan regulators on behalf of a political contributor, and one was accused of influence peddling—obtaining federal housing money in exchange for campaign donations. As both houses of Congress came under close scrutiny, political observers predicted there would be a wave of ethics reform.

Of special concern is the matter of *honoraria*, fees that members of Congress receive for speaking before special interest groups such as the Tobacco Institute and the Outdoor Advertising Association. Critics argue that honoraria create conflicts of interest. Legislators, after all, must deal with issues that can affect the interests of the groups that pay them these fees.

The Wright matter and the new concern with ethics revived the idea of a ban on appearance fees, and so, in one of the last acts of its 1989 session, Congress passed a package of ethics reforms. The law reduced

*Speaker of the House Jim Wright swears in the members of the U.S. House of Representatives as the 100th Congress convenes in January 1987. In May 1989, Wright resigned his post and his House seat after being charged with 69 violations of House ethics rules.*

honoraria limits and will prohibit them completely for House members in 1991; tightened rules on gifts, travel, reporting of assets, and lobbying; and raised pay for members of Congress, 1,115 federal judges, and 834 executive branch officials. Senators cannot keep more than $35,800 each year in such fees; House members can keep only $26,850. The rest usually is donated to charity. Since 1978, legislators have had to make public their financial holdings, gifts, and appearance fees. This new law attempted to counter the growing perception that the U.S. government has become "a government for sale." Whatever happens, ethics certainly will be one of the key campaign issues of the 1990s.

*Speaker of the House Thomas Foley relaxes in his office in Washington, D.C.*
*The Speaker, who presides over the conduct of the House's business, is the*
*legislative body's most powerful member. The Speaker also is traditionally*
*the leader of the majority party.*

Representatives is the *Speaker of the House*. The Speaker is elected at the
opening of each session of Congress by a caucus, or meeting, of all members
of the majority party—that is, the party, either Democratic or Republican, that
has won the most seats in the House. The Speaker presides over the business
of the House, recognizing (or ignoring) members who wish to speak. The
Speaker also appoints the chairperson and all members of the powerful Rules
Committee (which determines what bills are brought to the floor and how they
may be debated), appoints the members of the special committees that
periodically are created to conduct specific investigations, and refers proposed
legislation (bills) to particular committees for consideration. The Speaker is
also the political leader of the majority party in the House. Thus, the Speaker
simultaneously handles the formal job of moving legislation through the House
and the partisan task of attaining passage of the bills that his party favors. By
influencing (but not dictating) committee assignments and which bills come to
the House floor, the Speaker can reward party loyalty and punish disloyalty,
although not to the extent that once was possible. Today, the Speaker must be
equally skilled in parliamentary procedures and the art of gentle, yet firm,
persuasion.

The House *majority leader*, the Speaker's second in command, is a key party strategist who helps to schedule legislative debate and organizes the course of that debate on the floor of the House. The *majority whip*, who is assisted by a number of deputy whips, is responsible for keeping track of how party members will vote on important pieces of legislation and for attempting to win their support if they are leaning the "wrong" way. (The title is derived from whipper-in, the rider who keeps the hounds together during a fox hunt.) The minority party elects a *minority leader* and *minority whip*, who perform the same functions for their party.

The House Committee on Rules determines what bills are brought to the floor and how they may be debated. Without a "special rule" from the rules committee, no major legislative proposal can be considered by the House. The special rule determines whether there will be a time limit on debate and whether the bill may be amended. The entire House must vote to adopt each rule before it can go into effect.

Before a piece of proposed legislation can be debated and voted on by the full House, it must be placed on a *calendar*, a list of business eligible for consideration on the floor of the House. Bills that appropriate money or raise revenue are placed on the Union Calendar. Most bills that are not connected with appropriations go on the House Calendar. By far, the majority of House business is placed on these two calendars. Other calendars are: the Private Calendar, which deals with bills that affect private individuals (such as immigration matters); the Consent Calendar, which expedites noncontroversial bills to which fewer than 3 members object; and the Discharge Calendar, which lists motions to force a bill out of committee if they receive 218 signatures from House members (a procedure that rarely succeeds). After a bill is placed on the appropriate calendar, the rules committee sets the rules for debate on the floor. Only 16 percent of bills introduced in the House of Representatives ever reach the House floor.

# The Senate

The Senate is composed of 100 members, 2 from each of the 50 states. The Constitution requires that anyone elected to the Senate be at least 30 years of age, a citizen for at least 9 years, and an inhabitant of the state from which he or she is elected. Senators are elected on a statewide basis and serve a term of six years. Every two years one-third of the Senate must run for reelection.

*The document room of the House of Representatives contains printed copies of all bills (proposed legislation) in the various stages that they must go through before they become law.*

As stated in the Constitution, the vice-president is the "President of the Senate," responsible for presiding over the business of the body but votes only in the event of a tie. In reality, vice-presidents seldom attend Senate sessions. The *president pro tempore*, usually the member of the majority party with the most seniority in the Senate, is supposed to preside over the body in the vice-president's absence, but today this is more of an honorary position. The job of presiding over the day-to-day business of the Senate is rather tedious and normally is handled by junior members. Elected by the majority party caucus, the Senate *majority leader* is the most powerful member of the Senate and, because the position demands skill both as a lawmaker and a political leader, is very much like the Speaker of the House. The minority party in the Senate elects a *minority leader*. The two leaders generally work together to schedule votes on bills. In deference to their leadership and authority, during debates the presiding officer will call upon the majority and minority leaders before recognizing other senators.

The leader of each party is assisted by a whip, who, as in the House, is responsible for polling and rounding up party members for key votes. Senate whips also arrange vote pairing, in which a Senator agrees to cancel his or her vote by pairing it with an absent senator who would have voted the opposite way. Also, when the party leader is absent from the Senate, the whip stands in.

Because of its smaller size, the Senate lacks most of the strict procedures that govern business in the House. The Senate has only one legislative calendar. Bills usually are called up by unanimous consent; unless one senator objects, the bill is approved without amendment or debate. This procedure serves as a valuable time-saver because unlimited debate and wholesale amendments could bring Senate business to a standstill. The majority and minority leaders, therefore, will negotiate deals to avoid objections and achieve unanimous consent on most major bills. Without a unanimous consent agreement, however, the bill must be placed on the calendar and debated. One way of impeding the passage of a bill in the Senate is for opponents to propose large-scale, and often irrelevant, amendments, thus either stalling its progress or making it unattractive to a majority of the membership.

Unlike the House, where members usually can speak for no more than five minutes during debates, the Senate normally allows unlimited debate. As a result, a controversial bill may be the object of a delaying tactic known as a *filibuster*. A filibuster is a marathon speech in which a senator, or group of senators, literally tries to talk a bill to death. The idea is to tie up the bill—and

31

*The Senate chamber in the Capitol. The Constitution grants the Senate, the upper house of Congress, certain special powers: It has the sole authority to ratify treaties proposed by the president and to accept or reject presidential appointments to many government positions, including federal judgeships and cabinet posts.*

'YOU BACK AGAIN?'

*A cartoon satirizing the ability of a filibuster to defeat attempts to enact reform legislation. The filibuster, a delaying tactic that takes advantage of the Senate's rule of unlimited debate, potentially permits a minority of senators to stall a bill by talking endlessly and thereby preventing the Senate from taking action on it.*

the Senate—for so long that the bill never comes to a vote. As other bills pile up while the filibuster proceeds, the majority leader may have no choice but to send the bill back to committee, essentially killing it. To maintain a filibuster, all a senator has to do is talk and keep talking. After three hours the talk can be about anything. Senators have been known to read from Shakespeare, the Bible, and even the telephone book! When the first speaker gets tired he or she can yield to a colleague, and the filibuster continues. In this way, a filibuster can last for days, weeks, or months.

Since 1959, the procedure that can cut off a filibuster, known as *cloture*, has become somewhat easier. If three-fifths of the entire Senate (60 members) vote for cloture, the filibuster is stopped and business can proceed, at least in theory. But even with cloture, it is possible to exploit loopholes in the Senate rules and delay action through a post-cloture filibuster. Recently, time limits have been placed on post-cloture filibusters.

The filibuster traditionally is thought of as a tool that conservatives use to block progressive legislation. In 1957, for example, Senator Strom Thurmond of South Carolina filibustered against a civil rights bill for a solid 24 hours. The landmark Civil Rights Act of 1964—to cite just one of many examples—was passed only after a cloture vote ended a filibuster by southern conservatives. However, Senate liberals have employed this tactic as well, as in the early 1970s when they filibustered to prevent increased funding for the Vietnam War and the extension of the military draft. Whoever uses it, the filibuster is an effective way for a committed minority to block the efforts of the majority of the Senate.

# The Committee System

In 1885, future president Woodrow Wilson, then a distinguished political scientist, observed that Congress had become "government by the chairmen of the Standing Committees" and that it did little more than "sanction the decisions of its Committees as rapidly as possible." More than a hundred years later, most of the real nuts-and-bolts work of Congress is still done in the committees.

During a typical congressional session, nearly 10,000 bills—covering a range of issues as broad as the interests and concerns of the diverse American public—are introduced. No member of Congress could hope, or be expected, to be familiar with the specifics of every bill. The work has to be decentralized, divided up among the many members of Congress, each of whom becomes responsible for a small portion of the legislative branch's total work load. Therefore, each house of Congress is broken down into a collection of permanent *standing committees*, which consider bills and conduct hearings on specific legislative matters, such as foreign policy, agriculture, and education.

*The Senate Foreign Relations Committee holds a meeting in 1964. To manage its enormous work load, the Senate conducts its business through a committee system in which permanent committees and subcommittees consider bills and conduct hearings on specific matters. If a committee reports favorably on the bill it has considered, it presents the bill to the full Senate for approval.*

There are 22 standing committees in the House of Representatives and 16 in the Senate. Because virtually all new legislation introduced in Congress is referred to a committee, one of a committee's main functions is to screen bills that have little chance of becoming law.

The committee system has led to considerable specialization within Congress. Because the members of each committee are recognized as the resident experts in their area, the body as a whole tends to rely on their judgment. Once a committee has held hearings on, amended, and approved a bill, the Senate or House normally will defer to the committee's expertise and ratify its decision. Thus, the committee system is an effective and efficient means of handling a diverse and otherwise unwieldy work load.

In recent years, with an increase in the number of subcommittees, Congress has become even more decentralized. Subcommittees are superspecialists, small bodies formed out of the full committees to handle a particular detail or area within the committee's responsibility. By 1987, there were 152 subcommittees in the House and 92 in the Senate. The typical senator sits on 10 committees or subcommittees; the typical representative serves on at least 5.

The chairperson is the most influential member of the committee, with the power to call meetings, set agendas, and control the hiring, firing, and funding of the committee staff. The specialized knowledge that many chairs have amassed over the years is also a significant source of influence, both in and out of Congress. For example, it is generally agreed that no one on Capitol Hill—and perhaps in all of Washington—is more knowledgeable about defense matters than the chairperson of the Senate Armed Services Committee.

In the past, the much-criticized "seniority system" reigned absolute; the member with the longest period of service on the committee automatically occupied the chair. But since the early 1970s, the party caucuses in each house have voted to choose the committee chairpersons (if the party is in the majority) or ranking minority members (if it is in the minority). Although it is no longer the only factor, seniority is still the most important factor in selecting committee chairs—as late as 1988, the House has rejected seniority only four times, and the Senate never has.

In each house, the number of seats that a party has on the committees is proportional to the size of its delegation. Republican members receive their assignments through their party's Committee on Committees for either the House or the Senate. House Democrats are assigned to committees by the House Democratic Steering and Policy Committee, which, when the Democrats are in the majority, is chaired and greatly influenced by the Speaker. The Senate Democratic Steering Committee assigns Democrats in that chamber.

New members and members seeking changes in their committee assignment express their preferences to their party's selection committee. However, factors such as race, sex, geographical balance, occupation, and the views of senior committee members and the party leadership can determine a member's committee assignment. For example, a member who is not a lawyer would find it next to impossible to get assigned to the House or the Senate Judiciary Committee. Likewise, the increase in the number of women in the military was a major reason why, in 1973, Representative Patricia Schroeder of Colorado became the first woman assigned to the House Armed Services Committee.

Not all committee assignments are equally valued. Naturally, members want an assignment that allows them to work on the problems and concerns of their constituents back home. Assignments to the Budget or Appropriations Committees are prized because they provide the member of Congress with both an important lawmaking responsibility and the opportunity to allocate money to his

*In 1988, Representative Pat Schroeder of Colorado, a member of the House Armed Services Committee, speaks to reporters about electing a chairperson for the committee. Schroeder's assignment to the committee in 1973 reflected the needs and concerns of women, who were entering the military in record numbers.*

or her home district or state. Another important factor is media coverage. A seat on a highly visible committee, especially one dealing with the field of foreign policy, can help build a national reputation, an important consideration for any representative or senator who would like to be president someday.

In addition to the standing committees, temporary committees often are established for specific and limited purposes. At times Congress has created *select* or *special committees* to conduct investigations or resolve issues that have arisen. The Senate committee that in 1973 investigated wrongdoing in President Nixon's 1972 reelection campaign was a select committee. *Joint committees* comprise members of both the House and the Senate, such as the Joint Committee on Taxation. When the House and Senate versions of a particular bill differ, a *conference committee* made up of members of both houses is created to reconcile them.

# Congressional Support Agencies

The work of Congress is supported by four major agencies. The largest of these, the General Accounting Office (GAO), serves as a watchdog for waste or fraud in government, conducting investigations on behalf of congressional committees. In the 1980s, the GAO made headlines when it revealed that the Defense Department and other agencies had bought relatively inexpensive products, such as common hardware-store hammers, at far above their retail prices. The head of the GAO, the Comptroller General, is Congress's accountant, responsible for ensuring that funds are appropriately spent by the agencies and departments of the executive branch.

The Congressional Budget Office (CBO) provides Congress with an independent analysis of the president's annual budget and economic policies. Because it serves both parties, the CBO's economic forecasts are considered more reliable than those of the White House, which has a political stake in painting as rosy an economic picture as it can.

The Office of Technology Assessment helps Congress handle scientific and technological issues by conducting studies of such questions as the safety of nuclear reactors, the effects of Agent Orange exposure on Vietnam veterans, and the impact of computers on the individual's right to privacy.

Finally, within the Library of Congress—best known as a depository for a huge amount of printed and recorded material and so an indispensable reference resource for scholars in every field—is the Congressional Research Service. At the request of members of Congress, its 800-member research

*Library of Congress staff discuss a reference question in the U.S. Senate Reference Center. The Library of Congress, the national library of the United States, was created in 1800 to provide books for the use of Congress. The Library's Congressional Research Service, the reference and research arm of Congress, prepares reports on any subject for members.*

staff, with the assistance of a computerized data base, can carry out long-range studies or provide ready answers on a broad range of public policy issues.

## How a Bill Becomes a Law

Any member of Congress can introduce a bill. Except for tax or appropriations bills, which must originate in the House, a bill may be introduced in either chamber. Many bills are introduced in both houses simultaneously.

Once a bill is introduced, the Speaker or the presiding officer in the Senate refers it to a committee, which may hold hearings on the bill or assign it to one of its subcommittees for hearings. Except for matters of national security, hearings are usually open to the public. At these hearings, government officials, experts in the field, and concerned citizens testify for or against the bill. The subcommittee votes on the bill and reports its recommendation to the full committee. The committee may then either do nothing, "mark up" the bill (rewriting it substantially), or report the bill, either unchanged or in amended form, to the full chamber. The majority of all bills die in committee or subcommittee.

In the House, the bill then is placed on one of the five calendars, and the rules committee must issue a rule to determine the terms of debate. If no rule is issued, the bill dies. When debating a bill, the House often changes itself into the Committee of the Whole. It is still the full House, but the rules are less formal. As the Committee of the Whole, the number of representatives that must be present for the House to act, called a quorum, is only 100 members, rather than a majority. Once the allotted time for debate has expired, the Committee of the Whole turns back into the House, which then makes its final vote on the bill.

In the Senate, which has no rules committee, the bill is placed on the legislative calendar to await action. If a unanimous consent agreement has been reached, debate and amendments will be limited or dispensed with. If not, debate can run on indefinitely or until a vote for cloture can be achieved. Otherwise, the majority leader may have to return the bill to committee, killing it.

If a bill is introduced and passed in only one house, it then must be sent to the other house for hearings, reports, debates, and voting. The Constitution requires that both houses pass an identical bill before it can become law. So, all differences between the House and Senate versions of the bill must be resolved by a conference committee representing both houses and both parties. If a compromise can be reached by the conferees, both houses vote on it, and if both houses approve this final version of the bill it is sent to the president.

The president may sign the bill into law, let it become law without his signature, or he may veto it. Congress may override the president's veto by a two-thirds vote in each house, in which case the bill becomes law, but this occurs very infrequently. In a procedure known as a pocket veto, the president can also kill a bill by taking no action, if Congress adjourns during the 10-day period after the president receives the bill.

# The Budget-making Process

In 1974, the Congressional Budget and Impoundment Act established procedures for deciding how much money the government could spend in a fiscal year (which begins on October 1). On January 20 of each year, the president submits a proposed budget to Congress. The House and Senate budget committees, which were created by the 1974 law, consider the executive branch's requests, make their own recommendations, and report to their respective bodies a *budget resolution* that sets spending targets. Before the House of Representatives can consider specific spending bills, Congress must agree to this budget resolution.

# How a Bill Becomes Law

This chart illustrates how most proposed legislation is enacted.
There are easier and more elaborate paths through Congress,
and most bills never become law.

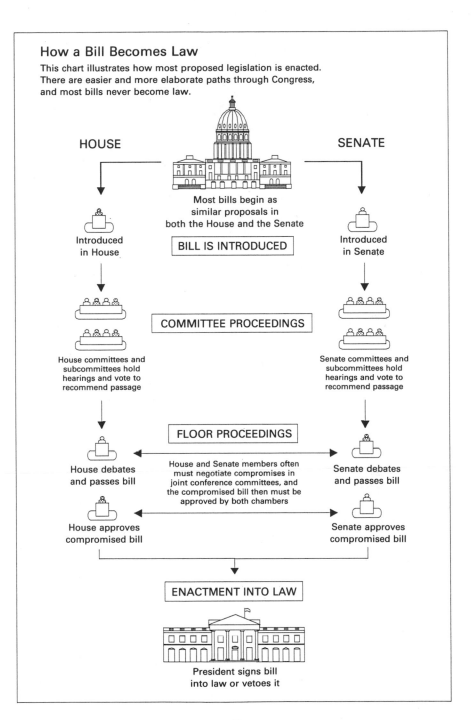

HOUSE

SENATE

Most bills begin as
similar proposals in
both the House and the Senate

Introduced
in House

**BILL IS INTRODUCED**

Introduced
in Senate

**COMMITTEE PROCEEDINGS**

House committees and
subcommittees hold
hearings and vote to
recommend passage

Senate committees and
subcommittees hold
hearings and vote to
recommend passage

**FLOOR PROCEEDINGS**

House debates
and passes bill

House and Senate members often
must negotiate compromises in
joint conference committees, and
the compromised bill then must be
approved by both chambers

Senate debates
and passes bill

House approves
compromised bill

Senate approves
compromised bill

**ENACTMENT INTO LAW**

President signs bill
into law or vetoes it

After the president submits a budget, each agency's or department's *authorization*—its legal authority to operate at a specific level of funding—is reviewed by the relevant standing committees in the House and Senate. For example, the authorized funding level for the Department of Defense is reviewed by the Senate and House Armed Services Committees. The authorizing committee can accept the agency's funding request, enlarge it, or reduce it.

Then the appropriations committees in both houses review each agency's *appropriation*, a grant of money to fund the agency, and make recommendations on the entire budget. Generally, the appropriations committee's recommendations are lower than the amounts suggested by the various authorizing committees. This is because individual standing committees tend to develop close ties to the agencies and departments that they oversee, while the appropriations committees are able to remain somewhat more detached and objective. Because only the appropriations committees can determine actual spending, their figures carry more weight.

Authorization and appropriations bills both have to pass each house, and, as with all legislation, differences between House and Senate versions must be resolved in a conference. When the president signs the budget bill, the federal government can continue operating for another fiscal year. Sometimes, Congress fails to create a budget by the October 1 start of the fiscal year and has to enact temporary emergency funding measures to keep the government in business until it agrees on a new budget. In 1985, responding to growing budget deficits, which happen when the federal government spends more money than it has in the Treasury, Congress passed the Balanced Budget Act (better known as the Gramm-Rudman-Hollings Act). The act set annually decreasing deficit limits, or "ceilings," that by 1991 would have been reduced to zero (at which time, the budget would be balanced). The bill required unprecedented automatic budget cuts in any year when the deficit rose above the specified level.

However, the Supreme Court in 1986 ruled that because the cuts would have been enforced by the Comptroller General, an official who can be removed by Congress, the Gramm-Rudman-Hollings Act encroached on the constitutional authority of the president. Congress rewrote the law in 1987, pushing back the deadline for a balanced budget to 1993 and giving the power to make budget cuts to the Office of Management and Budget, an agency within the executive branch.

*Richard Darman, director of the executive branch's Office of Management and Budget (OMB), testifies before the Senate Finance Committee in March 1989. Congress has empowered the OMB to make cuts in the federal government's budget in order to balance it.*

# Congress and Foreign Policy

The Constitution divides the power to conduct foreign and military affairs between Congress and the president. The president nominates ambassadors and commands the armed forces. Congress has the power to declare war and appropriate money for defense, and the Senate approves or rejects treaties and ambassadorial nominations.

In practice, however, the boundary between congressional and presidential authority is far from clear cut. Since the end of the Second World War, presidents have conducted two full-scale wars (in Korea and Vietnam) and authorized invasions of several foreign countries (such as Cuba, Grenada, and Panama) without a declaration of war from Congress. As a response to the threat of nuclear conflict and a perceived, if not always actual, need for increased security, Congress has allowed the president broad autonomy in foreign and military affairs.

At the end of World War II, *bipartisanship*, the idea that it is in the national interest for both parties to support the president's foreign policy, prevailed in Congress. This notion was expressed most succinctly by Senator Arthur H. Vandenberg of Michigan in 1950: "Politics stops at the water's edge." The heyday of bipartisanship was the early 1950s, when the Republican Vandenberg chaired the Senate Foreign Relations Committee, and Harry S. Truman, a Democrat, was president; however, the idea has survived through the 1980s. In 1989, for example, the Democrat-controlled Congress overwhelmingly approved a request from President Bush, a Republican, for $49.75 million in nonmilitary, so-called humanitarian, aid to the "contras," right-wing rebels who had waged a 10-year war against the Sandinista government in Nicaragua. Speaker Jim Wright, a notoriously partisan Democrat, hailed Bush's aid program as "a chance for a new beginning" in Nicaragua.

Perhaps the most well-known instance of Congress having abdicated its authority in foreign policy occurred in 1964, when American ships stationed in the Gulf of Tonkin reportedly were attacked by North Vietnam. At President Johnson's request, Congress passed the Tonkin Gulf Resolution, which gave him the power "to take all necessary measures" to repel the attack and prevent further aggression. Only two senators, and no representatives, voted against the resolution. President Johnson, and later President Nixon, used the resolution as blanket permission to escalate and prolong the war, even after Congress repealed it in 1970. It later turned out that reports of the attack were exaggerated; Congress, and the nation, paid dearly for its willingness to yield so uncritically to the wishes of the president.

By the early 1970s, more and more Americans realized that the Vietnam War was a losing cause. In 1973, Congress attempted to reassert its authority

*U.S. troops patrol a street in Grenada during a 1983 invasion of the Caribbean island. Although the Constitution vests in Congress the sole power to declare war and appropriate money for the military, several presidents have extended their constitutional authority as commander in chief of the armed forces to direct invasions of other nations to achieve limited military or political goals.*

*Ousted Panamanian dictator Manuel Noriega poses for a Justice Department mug shot in Miami, Florida, on January 4, 1990, after being brought to the United States to face drug trafficking charges. Noriega surrendered to the U.S. troops that had invaded Panama on orders by President George Bush to capture him.*

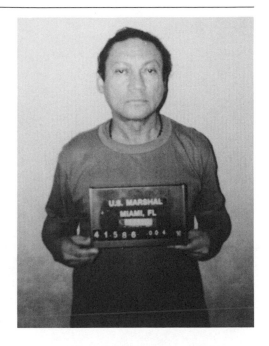

in foreign affairs and prevent future Vietnam-like situations by passing, over Nixon's veto, the War Powers Act. This act requires the president to notify Congress of any use of troops abroad and limits their commitment in foreign countries to 60 days, unless Congress declares war or issues a special authorization.

Nevertheless, Presidents Ford and Carter ordered military actions without first notifying Congress. President Reagan insisted that he reported the invasion of Grenada to Congress voluntarily, not because the War Powers Act required him to do so. In December 1989, President Bush ordered the invasion of Panama to capture its president, General Manuel Noriega, and return him to the United States to face drug-trafficking charges.

While it may have prevented them from committing the nation to prolonged, Vietnam-like military involvements, the law has not stopped presidents from sending troops abroad without the consent of Congress. The ineffectiveness of the War Powers Act testifies to the relative strength of the presidency versus Congress in foreign affairs.

*Richard Nixon launches his 1968 presidential campaign with a parade in Chicago's business district. The Constitution requires that the president be at least 35 years old and a natural-born citizen of the United States.*

# THREE

# The Presidency

Article II of the Constitution stipulates that the president must be at least 35 years old and a natural-born citizen of the United States. The president serves a term of four years. Although the Constitution originally did not limit the number of terms to which a president may be elected, George Washington established the custom of serving two terms only—a tradition that continued until the presidency of Franklin Roosevelt, who was elected to four terms. The Twenty-second Amendment, ratified in 1951, now limits presidents to two terms.

## The Many Roles of the President

It is said that the president wears many hats. This is a bit misleading, for although the president does play many roles, they are not so neatly compartmentalized in practice as they seem to be in theory. Further, the president's roles not only tend to overlap but at times also conflict. For analytical purposes, however, it is convenient to separate the various roles that the president must play.

As *chief executive*, the president heads a huge governmental organization, or bureaucracy, and he is ultimately responsible for its actions. (Chief bureaucrat,

47

*President Reagan (left), First Lady Nancy Reagan (center), and Diana, Princess of Wales (right), make their way to a state dinner in 1985. One of the roles that the president performs is that of chief of state, serving as the nation's representative at various social functions.*

therefore, may be a more accurate term.) As the sign on President Truman's desk said, "The buck stops here." Because he has the power under the Constitution to recommend legislation to Congress, as well as to veto laws that Congress has passed, the president can be thought of as the *chief legislator*. Active, large-scale participation in the legislative process is a practice of modern presidents, but even in George Washington's day, many of the laws passed by Congress were written by the president and his staff.

As *commander in chief* of the armed forces, the president has authority over both military personnel and the conduct of military actions. Civilian supremacy over the military is a fundamental constitutional principle. In April 1951, during the Korean War, President Truman dismissed General Douglas MacArthur because of the general's continued attempts to exceed his authority and extend the war into China. MacArthur, however, had a strong political following and a flair for dramatic rhetoric, and the president soon found himself under intense pressure from a large segment of Congress and the voters. Still, Truman was certain that his action, although unpopular, was constitutionally sound: "I fired him because he wouldn't respect the authority of the President." Over the years, history has judged Truman to have been correct.

The president is the *chief diplomat*, the primary architect of the nation's foreign policy and its spokesperson in negotiations with other countries. Frequently the president must also act as *chief of state*, the ceremonial head of the government who represents the nation and its people through a variety of social duties, such as hosting state dinners for foreign dignitaries and honoring outstanding citizens for their contributions to the arts and sciences.

By virtue of his high office, the president is *chief of the party*, his party's top politician. Some presidents, such as Truman and Reagan, relished their partisan role; others, such as Eisenhower, found it distasteful. Nevertheless, as John F. Kennedy observed, "No president . . . can escape politics."

# The Growth of Presidential Power

To paraphrase George Orwell's *Animal Farm*, all the branches of the federal government are equal, but some branches are more equal than others. The executive branch, which is headed by the president, is the "most equal" of the three. This was not what the authors of the Constitution had in mind. They envisioned the position as a kind of presiding officer for the government. Still, according to their Constitution, the president's powers were not so much restricted as they were vague. It was left to the individuals who held the office and the uncontrollable twists and turns of history to define the presidency in practice.

Even the reluctant first president, George Washington, chosen unanimously by the electors to two terms (1789–97), believed that his authority extended beyond what was stated explicitly in Article II. He expanded the institutions of the executive branch, created a national bank, took an active role in developing legislation, and established the role of the presidency in foreign policy. Most importantly, Washington's charisma and leadership helped build respect, in the United States and abroad, for the American "experiment." Because of Washington, the presidency became the personal embodiment of the nation.

With notable exceptions, most presidents from the 1800s to the early 1900s were able men, but neither strong nor innovative national leaders. The few exceptional presidents, however, left a permanent mark on the office. Although he did not consider the office, or his performance in it, very important, Thomas Jefferson (1801–9) began the continental expansion of the United States through the Louisiana Purchase. Andrew Jackson (1829–37) took an adversarial posture toward Congress. Unlike previous executives, who vetoed only legislation they believed was unconstitutional, Jackson was the first president to veto laws that he did not like, a prerogative that contemporary presidents argue is both natural and necessary. Theodore Roosevelt (1901–9) expanded American involvement in foreign affairs and, for better or for worse, established the president's power to send troops to intervene in other countries.

The framers of the Constitution did not specify the precise boundaries of presidential authority. They left room for innovation and expansion of the office, as conditions might require. They seemed to realize, if only intuitively, that the success or failure of the new nation would depend on the ability of the president to act, without undue restriction, as the nation's leader.

During the administration of Abraham Lincoln (1861–65) this notion was borne out in practice. With divisions between North and South threatening to tear the nation apart, Lincoln resolutely maintained that individual states, however much they disagreed with the actions of the federal government, could not leave the Union. He backed his reading of the Constitution with military force, at great human cost to both sides. In the end, however, the Union was preserved. During this grave chapter in American history, Lincoln demonstrated that among the branches of government, only the presidency could respond decisively to urgent national crises. But once the civil conflict was resolved, the presidency reverted to its traditional low profile.

In the 20th century, the conditions of a changing nation in a changing world have permanently altered the character of the presidency and, thus, the balance of power in Washington. In the course of responding to national crises, the modern presidency has evolved into its current form. A world war in the 1910s, the near collapse of the national—and world—economy in the 1930s, another world war in the 1940s, and more than four decades of political conflict and cold war with the Soviet bloc have entrenched the executive branch in the

BORN TO COMMAND.

OF VETO MEMORY.

HAD I BEEN CONSULTED.

KING ANDREW THE FIRST.

*President Andrew Jackson (1829–37) was regarded as a tyrant by his political adversaries. This cartoon satirizes "King Andrew" as he uses the veto power to trample on the Constitution, the judiciary, and the Bank of the United States (marked as "internal improvements"). Jackson fought vigorously with both Congress and the Supreme Court, and he was the first president to veto laws that he disliked.*

51

forefront of national politics. War and peace, boom and bust—these are national issues requiring national policies and national leadership. The president, the only nationally elected official, is in a unique position to provide that leadership and create those policies.

For example, President Franklin Roosevelt (1933–45) insisted that the Great Depression of the 1930s called for bold federal action. With the economy in ruins, he initiated a package of legislative reforms, known as the New Deal, that was designed to turn the nation back toward economic prosperity. For the first time, the federal government assumed the responsibility for managing the nation's economy. Today the legacy of the New Deal can be seen in programs such as Medicare and Social Security, as well as a whole range of regulations in the fields of banking, industry, and labor relations. Moreover, post–New Deal presidents are not charged merely with engineering recovery when economic collapses occur; rather, they must make sure that such collapses never happen.

Thus, the development of this once-tiny, farm-based republic into a world military and economic power has compelled American presidents since Woodrow Wilson (1913–21) to accept responsibilities that the authors of the Constitution probably did not envision but nevertheless did not prohibit. There have been times, however, when presidents may have gone too far in the exercise and enlargement of their power. The question often is raised, "Is the expansion of presidential power always necessary and legitimate?" Political historian Arthur M. Schlesinger, jr., has noted the emergence of what he calls "the imperial presidency," the tendency for presidents, especially in foreign and military affairs, to exceed their constitutional bounds and usurp the legitimate authority of Congress.

Presidents enjoy a particular capacity to raise and focus (and sometimes to blur) issues in the consciousness of the American public. They frequently are able to justify their actions by appealing to the public's fear of crisis. After all, crises demand decisive and speedy mobilization, an ability that is generally believed to be incorporated in the presidency. Realizing this, presidents have been known to create crises.

Postwar chief executives have propagated the notion of "permanent crisis," repeatedly raising the threat of communist expansion, real or imagined, to justify interventions, military or covert, in foreign counties. During the Eisenhower administration (1953–61), the Central Intelligence Agency (CIA) helped overthrow elected leaders in Guatemala and Iran, replacing them with dictatorial regimes that were friendlier to American interests. America's

*The first recipient of Social Security retirement benefits, 91-year-old Ida Fuller of Ludlow, Vermont. Many social welfare programs, such as Social Security, originated during the New Deal, a package of legislative reforms introduced by President Franklin D. Roosevelt in the 1930s to help the nation recover from the Great Depression.*

On August 5, 1964, Secretary of Defense Robert McNamara points to the spot in the Gulf of Tonkin where two U.S. destroyers were allegedly attacked by North Vietnamese torpedo boats. McNamara announced that U.S. naval aircraft were conducting retaliatory raids against North Vietnamese military bases. Congress later issued the Tonkin Gulf Resolution, supporting the U.S. raids and authorizing the president to pursue any other "necessary" military measures.

military commitment to, and escalation of, the war in Vietnam was founded on the Johnson administration's exaggerated report of a 1964 North Vietnamese attack on American ships in the Gulf of Tonkin. And it is questionable whether American medical students really were in danger when in 1983 President Reagan invaded Grenada "to protect American lives," toppling its leftist government in the process.

The imperial presidency has created a dilemma for contemporary American politics. Should the power of the presidency be allowed to grow unchecked, or should it be severely curtailed? Schlesinger suggests that there must be "a middle ground," that the president should be neither a "czar" nor a "puppet." In this 20th-century world, a strong president is almost certainly a necessity, but, he notes, this should be "a strong Presidency *within the Constitution.*"

# The Cabinet

The cabinet is an informal body consisting of the president, the vice-president, the heads of the 14 departments of the executive branch (such as State,

*President Lyndon B. Johnson meets with his cabinet in April 1967. The cabinet is an informal body composed of the heads of executive branch departments, such as the secretary of state, who advise the president on many important issues.*

Defense, Justice, and Housing and Urban Development) and certain other senior officials (such as the director of the CIA). The Constitution does not provide for a cabinet, and no law requires the president to form one.

The idea of an advisory body to help a leader make decisions goes all the way back to the political theories of the Greek philosopher Aristotle (384–322 B.C.). In the United States, however, its usefulness has been debated as far back as the earliest days of the new nation. Benjamin Franklin believed that a cabinet "would not only be a check on a bad President but be a relief to a good one." Alexander Hamilton argued that, on the contrary, the cabinet would prove to be either "a clog upon his good intentions" or "a cloak to conceal his faults."

Presidents use one of two basic models in selecting a cabinet. Abraham Lincoln chose his cabinet for its political value, appointing two defeated political rivals, Salmon P. Chase and William H. Seward, as secretaries of the Treasury and state, respectively. As a result, Lincoln's cabinet was one of the most politically competent and influential in history. Woodrow Wilson assembled his cabinet from men whom he found intellectually capable and compatible with himself. The problem was that although this group may have been collectively one of the most brilliant of all cabinets, it was politically unknown and inexperienced.

Most presidents strike a balance between political and intellectual consider- ations in selecting their cabinets. In some of his cabinet appointments President Bush, for example, looked outside of government to find top people in their fields, such as Dr. Louis Sullivan, whom he appointed as secretary of health and human services. Bush filled other cabinet posts with Republican party leaders and political rivals, such as Jack Kemp as secretary of housing and urban development and Elizabeth Dole as secretary of labor.

Historically, the cabinet has been of little value in helping presidents to see issues clearly or to influence the political arena more effectively. Kennedy thought cabinet meetings were a waste of time. Johnson never discussed the conduct of the Vietnam War with his cabinet. During his beleaguered second term, with the Watergate scandal engulfing his presidency, Nixon rarely sought the advice of his cabinet members.

Even presidents who, as a rule, tend to rely on their cabinets, do not feel bound by them. Carter met more frequently with his cabinet than any president since Eisenhower; yet, during one week in 1979 he fired or accepted the resignation of five of its members. Even Lincoln, who built a strong and exceptional cabinet, recognized that the body tends to exist in a political limbo.

*Elizabeth Dole, President George Bush's secretary of labor. Presidents often appoint leading members of their own party to positions in their cabinet.*

Once, when his cabinet unanimously disagreed with him, Lincoln counted up the votes: "Seven nays, one aye—the ayes have it."

Why has the cabinet been of so little value as an adviser to the president? The answer lies in the nature of the institution. Simply put, the only thing cabinet members have in common is that they belong to the same administration. In terms of policy questions, they have very little to say to each other and for good reason. It is not the secretary of agriculture's job to advise the commander in chief on military strategy. And what does the secretary of defense know about farm price-support policy? In order to be able to debate a broad range of national policies, the cabinet would have to be made up of experienced and versatile students of American politics. This is rarely the case.

Furthermore, cabinet members tend to be influenced by the narrow interests of the department that they head. These parochial, bureaucratic concerns can color the advice that they give to the president. Moreover, the heads of competing departments are likely to offer conflicting views, none of which may take into account the larger picture. For this reason, Vice-president Charles G. Dawes (1925–29) lamented, "The members of the Cabinet are a President's natural enemies."

Because he could not find "the necessary standards of selflessness and candor" in his cabinet, Andrew Jackson turned to an inner circle of personal advisers, his so-called Kitchen Cabinet. Since then, most presidents have consulted trusted friends and longtime political allies who may not hold a position in the cabinet but nevertheless function as key policy advisers. Reagan, for example, promised in the 1980 campaign to institute a cabinet government, but when he was elected, he relied far more on a small group of White House aides and political associates from his days as governor of California.

## The Executive Office of the President

Twentieth-century presidents rely on large staffs. Today, a minibureaucracy of aides, policy advisers, speech writers, and liaisons exists within the White House. In fiscal year 1989, the Office of Personnel Management listed 377 people under the "White House Office," with a budget of nearly $28 million.

It was not always this way. George Washington paid a nephew out of his own pocket to be his only full-time aide. Congress did not appropriate funding for a presidential clerk until 1857. Lincoln often opened and answered the White

House mail himself, and Grover Cleveland, in the 1880s, answered the White House telephone!

Of course, only a handful of the White House staff occupy positions of real influence over policy matters. But those that do often rival and even overwhelm the ability of cabinet members to catch the president's ear. For example, Nixon's national security adviser, Henry Kissinger, emerged as the most powerful voice in foreign affairs, whereas Secretary of State William Rogers became the administration's forgotten man. Nixon eventually named Kissinger secretary of state. Two of Reagan's original White House staff members, Edwin Meese III, counsel to the president, and James A. Baker III, White House chief of staff, were appointed to the cabinet in Reagan's second term—Baker as secretary of the Treasury and Meese as attorney general.

The chief of staff is the key position in any White House. He serves as the president's gatekeeper, the guardian of the Oval Office who decides what matters and which individuals will be allowed to occupy the president's scarce

*Secretary of State James Baker III testifies before the Senate Appropriations Committee in April 1989. Baker served previously as White House chief of staff and secretary of the Treasury during President Ronald Reagan's administration.*

time. The chief of staff also serves as the president's buffer, the person who takes the heat when people do not get what they want from the president.

After the chief of staff, the president's press secretary performs the second most important job in the White House, arranging press conferences and briefings and speaking directly to the press on behalf of the president. In other words, the press secretary projects—and to a large extent creates—the image that newspapers, radio, and most importantly, television present of the president, an enormous responsibility in this media age.

The way a president selects and uses his staff varies with the temperament of the person in the Oval Office. Franklin Roosevelt encouraged a level of "creative chaos" by choosing a staff of versatile generalists, each possessing a broad range of experience and talents, who could develop and present to him competing policy alternatives. Eisenhower, on the other hand, was a former general and wanted his staff to be a civilian version of the military chain of command, with competent specialists who kept to their own areas and out of each other's way, and a chief of staff who determined what he should see.

Kennedy was more like Roosevelt in that he viewed his staff as a wheel and a series of spokes with himself at the hub. Johnson, a demanding and somewhat insecure personality, preferred to surround himself with a staff of yes-men that deferred to his authority. Nixon allowed himself to be isolated behind White House gates that were carefully guarded by his formidable chief, H. R. Haldeman. Reagan let advisers compete, often publicly, to influence him; the losers in these debates might wind up leaving the administration, while the winner's prestige grew in the president's eyes.

The White House office is only a small part of what is known as the Executive Office of the President. Established in 1939, today it consists of a group of councils and offices with a total staff of around 1,600 and a combined budget for fiscal 1989 of $125 million. Its two most important agencies are the Office of Management and Budget (OMB) and the National Security Council (NSC).

The OMB was created in 1970 to assist the president by performing two key functions. First, it oversees the operations of the executive branch, monitoring when federal agencies spend their budget allocations, what they do with their funds, what new policy ideas they develop, and how effectively and efficiently they operate. Second, the OMB prepares the federal budget that the president submits each year to Congress, advising him on how funds should be allocated among the competing departments, agencies, and programs of the executive branch.

*Zbigniew Brzezinski (left) who headed the National Security Council (NSC) under President Jimmy Carter, meets with the president in the Oval Office of the White House in January 1977. The NSC helps the president coordinate foreign, military, and intelligence policies.*

The NSC, created in 1947, helps the president coordinate foreign, military, and intelligence policy. By law, its members are the president, vice-president, and secretaries of state and defense, but it also can include the director of the CIA, the chairman of the Joint Chiefs of Staff, and other officials on whom the president might rely. The president's national security adviser directs the NSC staff, who provide the background research that the council uses in the formulation of the nation's foreign policy.

Different presidents have made varying uses of the NSC and its staff. Eisenhower relied on it extensively. However, Kennedy, during the 1962 Cuban missile crisis, consulted a larger, informal body of advisers instead of the NSC. Under Nixon, and directed by Kissinger, it was far more important than the State Department. In the Reagan administration, secret arms sales to Iran and the illegal use of the profits from these sales to aid the contras in Nicaragua—the "Iran-contra scandal"—were conducted by an NSC staff member, Marine Lieutenant Colonel Oliver North.

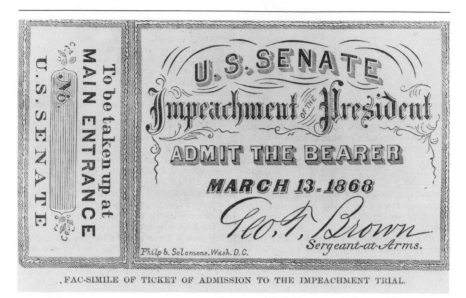

*A ticket to President Andrew Johnson's impeachment trial in 1868. The House of Representatives exercised its right to bring charges against the president. After a three-month trial, the Senate acquitted Johnson by a margin of one vote.*

Of the other agencies that come under the umbrella of the Executive Office of the President, one of the most important is the Office of Policy Development, which assists the president in formulating domestic policy in such fields as agriculture, commerce and trade, health, energy, natural resources, and drug abuse. The Council of Economic Advisers is a three-member panel of professional economists that is supposed to give impartial advice to the president on questions of national economic policy. When the council's chair, Martin Feldstein, resigned in 1984 after frequently criticizing the Reagan administration's policy, some members of the president's staff urged that he abolish the council after his reelection. Although Reagan did not follow their advice, the situation indicates the kind of political pressures to which even supposedly impartial advisers are subjected.

## The Reality of Presidential Power

In January 1787, in a letter to George Washington, John Jay pondered the structure of the new Constitution; "Shall we have a king?" he mused. If Jay were to return today, he might wonder, "Do we have a king?" At first glance, modern presidents may appear to exert a level of influence over domestic and foreign affairs that would be the envy of Old World monarchs. Upon closer examination, however, the picture is much less clear. An observation made in 1939 by British political commentator Harold Laski seems more to the point: "The President of the United States is both more and less than a king."

The Constitution, of course, places limits on the power of the presidency. Congress can override a president's veto with a two-thirds vote in each house. The Senate can reject his nominees for cabinet posts, positions on the federal and Supreme courts, ambassadorships, and other important administration jobs. And his *executive orders*, policy decisions issued during emergencies and having the authority of law, may be ruled unconstitutional by the Supreme Court.

Then there is the ultimate restraint on the president—*impeachment*. According to the Constitution, a president can be removed from office if he has committed "Treason, Bribery or other high Crimes and Misdemeanors." By a majority vote, the House of Representatives can impeach the president, that is, charge him with crimes, much like an indictment in a criminal proceeding. He is then tried by the Senate with the chief justice of the Supreme Court presiding. A two-thirds vote is required to convict the president and remove him from office.

In 1868, President Andrew Johnson was impeached and escaped removal from office by just one vote. The only other president to face imminent

*President Richard Nixon announces his resignation on August 8, 1974. Nixon faced an impending House vote on articles of impeachment for his role in obstructing the investigation of the break-in of the Democratic National Committee at the Watergate office complex by burglars working for his 1972 reelection committee.*

63

impeachment was Richard Nixon. On June 17, 1972, members of Nixon's reelection committee broke into the Democratic party's national headquarters in the Watergate office building in Washington, D.C., an event that became known as the notorious Watergate affair. In the summer of 1974, the House Judiciary Committee voted three articles of impeachment against Nixon, charging that he had attempted to conceal the burglary. Wisely, Nixon resigned before the full House could act on the charges.

Along with these specific constitutional provisions, there are a number of institutional limits on the power of the president. As Kennedy observed, "It is very easy to defeat a bill in the Congress. It is much more difficult to pass one." The ability of the president to function effectively as "chief legislator" depends upon the cooperation of Congress, a particularly frustrating condition when one or both houses is controlled by the opposition party. And even members of Congress from the president's party have to worry about their own constituencies, whose concerns may be narrower than or conflict with the national interests that the president is supposed to represent.

The president may even have a difficult time ruling his own executive branch. The federal bureaucracy is supposed to carry out his policies and decisions, but it often seems that the bureaucracy runs the president, rather than vice versa. Bureaucracies are notoriously slow in responding to demands for change, a constant source of frustration for presidents. Truman was amused at the thought of his successor, former general Eisenhower, trying to deal with this bureaucratic inertia: "He'll say, 'Do this! Do that!' *And nothing will happen.* Poor Ike—it won't be a bit like the army."

Political scientist Richard Neustadt, who also served as a consultant to the Kennedy administration, in 1960 concluded that presidential power is, in fact, "the power to persuade." Obviously the president needs the support of legislators, bureaucrats, and judges, but they also need him. This gives the president the ability to bargain and barter with these other key Washington policymakers. The most effective kind of president is one who can build coalitions by persuading those who hold other positions of power to support him.

The president is in a unique position to dispense favors to his allies and punish those who abandon him. He can reward his friends in a variety of ways, for example, by campaigning for them when they are up for reelection or requesting budgetary appropriations for projects in their home districts. On the other hand, legislators can feel the president's wrath if they refuse to back him. A Reagan aide described, metaphorically, how the administration changed the mind of one Republican senator who was about to vote against the president:

*Press photographers shoot President Ronald Reagan's meeting with members of Congress to discuss his economic recovery proposals. Since the 1960s, presidents have used the mass media—especially television—to build public opinion in their favor.*

"We stood him in front of an open grave and told him he could jump in if he wanted to."

But despite the arm-twisting, budgetary blackmail, and threats of political punishment, the president's real ability to persuade often rests more on his personal popularity than on his powers, constitutional or otherwise. The president must be able to enlist public support for his programs. Presidents who are able to use the mass media to shape public opinion in their favor enjoy an advantage in the Washington political arena. This is why the president's approval rating can be an important gauge of his ability to govern effectively. Legislators may see few benefits in supporting the programs of a president who is unpopular with the voters.

The complex reality of presidential power was summed up in the mid-1970s by political commentator Emmet John Hughes: "The President—*any* President—has some power to do almost anything, absolute power to do a few things, but never full power to do all things."

# The Vice-presidency

John Adams, the first vice-president, said it best: "I am Vice President. In this I am nothing, but I may be everything." The vice-president becomes president in the event of the incumbent's death, resignation, or removal from office. This has occurred nine times in the nation's history, eight times through death and once through resignation. For this reason it is said that the vice-president "is a heartbeat away" from the presidency.

Originally, the Constitution provided that each elector was to cast two votes for the president, choosing from a single field of names that included both the presidential candidates and their vice-presidential running mate. The person with the most votes became president, and the person with the second most became vice-president—regardless of either party affiliation or the office they actually were seeking. In other words, it was possible for members of different parties to be elected president and vice-president and for the vice-presidential candidate to be elected president.

In 1796, John Adams, a Federalist, was chosen president, and Thomas Jefferson, his opponent from the rival Democratic-Republican party, became vice-president. An even stranger situation occurred in the 1800 election, when Jefferson and his vice-presidential running mate, Aaron Burr, tied for the presidency. After 36 ballots and much turmoil, the House of Representatives, which decides tied presidential elections, selected Jefferson. The 1796 and 1800 elections exposed flaws in the electoral process, resulting in the 1804 adoption of the Twelfth Amendment, which provides that separate ballots be cast for the two offices. The person who

*John Adams, the first vice-president of the United States.*

is elected president is now guaranteed a vice-president from the same party.

Other than succeeding the president, the office has few formal duties. Vice-presidents can preside over the Senate, which they rarely do, and cast the deciding vote in case of a tie, which seldom happens but can be crucial when it does. Under the Twenty-fifth Amendment, the vice-president helps decide whether the president is "unable to discharge the powers and duties of his office," and if so, becomes "acting president." Obviously, this would occur only in unusual and extreme situations.

Vice-presidents seldom are given a central role in the administration. They make speeches (usually on noncontroversial topics), head presidential commissions on such subjects as drugs or space exploration (but take little part in their day-to-day functioning), and act as goodwill ambassadors overseas. The typical vice-president is more a public relations figure than a key adviser or confidant to the president.

Franklin Roosevelt told the first of his three vice-presidents, John Nance Garner, "You tend to your office, and I'll tend to mine." Vice-president Spiro Agnew did little more than lead the Nixon administration's attacks on liberals, antiwar protestors, and the press. George Bush, who for eight years was barely visible in the Reagan White House, provided an easy target at the 1988 Democratic Convention; in his speech to the delegates, Senator Edward Kennedy asked repeatedly, "Where was George?" Even Walter Mondale, who under President Carter had more responsibility than did most vice-presidents, lamented that he was not as well known as was the president's daughter, Amy.

Perhaps the reason that vice-presidents quickly become Washington's "invisible men" is that they are chosen more for their political value than for their qualifications and talents. The vice-presidential candidate is used to "balance the ticket," that is, to build support among a segment of the voters for which the presidential nominee may have little appeal. And so, the two candidates on a party's ticket frequently hail from separate geographic regions and may represent different ideological wings of their party. The most recent example of this occurred on the 1988 Democratic ticket, when the liberal governor of Massachusetts, Michael Dukakis, ran with Senator Lloyd Bentsen, a conservative Texan.

Clearly, it would make sense for the presidential nominee to select a running mate who is experienced, capable, and ideologically compatible. Likewise, there is good reason for presidents to give their vice-president a key role in their administration—after all, in this century alone, seven vice-presidents have become president, either through a president's death or resignation or their own election.

*A cartoon satirizes the power of the bureaucracy. Many people—from presidents who have been unable to control the bureaucracy to citizens who have been stymied in their dealings with it—complain about the unresponsiveness and inefficiency of the federal bureaucracy.*

"Think of it! Presidents come and go, but WE go on forever!" (© 1976 by NEA, Inc. Reprinted by permission)

# FOUR

# The Federal Bureaucracy

In modern society, people deal with bureaucracy almost constantly. Industries, labor unions, schools, religious institutions, banks, insurance companies, department stores, sports leagues—all of these are run by bureaucracies. And of course, bureaucracy exists at every level of government. To most Americans bureaucracy is a dirty word. It conjures up nightmarish images— hordes of desperate people filling out complicated and meaningless forms, waiting in line to see impersonal, faceless clerks, being shuttled through gray, mazelike corridors from one office to another, finding no relief, just more red tape. To label someone a bureaucrat is to utter the worst kind of insult.

Politicians, particularly when they are running for an office they do not yet occupy, have found that bureaucracy, or "big government," is a convenient catchall for the nation's problems and an easy way to attack the incumbent. At the same time, incumbents can blame the bureaucracy for the failures of their own programs—"It was a good idea, until the bureaucrats got their hands on it. . . ." It seems that all a politician has to do is cry "Bureaucracy, bureaucracy!" and the voters recoil with fear and loathing.

# A Necessary Evil?

In the midst of all the antibureaucratic passion and bombast, it is necessary to understand what a bureaucracy really is. In the simplest terms, bureaucracy is synonymous with administration. It refers to the way that large organizations attempt to coordinate the activities of its members in order to attain a common goal. *Public administration* is the term used to describe the operations of the government bureaucracy, the process by which government fulfills its diverse functions and puts its many and varied programs and policies into practice.

According to German sociologist Max Weber (1864–1920), all bureaucracies share certain features. First, they are organized in hierarchies, with authority flowing from the top down. Second, one's position within that hierarchy tends to reflect his or her expertise, experience, and—most importantly—power and prestige. Inequality is an inherent characteristic of bureaucracies. Third, bureaucracies are governed by a strict system of rules and regulations. Weber argued that the power of a bureaucracy is based upon its expertise and ability to apply technical knowledge to a particular task. Because they lack the specialized training of the bureaucrat, politicians can be at a disadvantage in their dealings with the bureaucracy. "The absolute monarch," Weber wrote, "is powerless opposite the superior knowledge of the bureaucratic expert."

Many of the criticisms that have been leveled against bureaucracies are well founded. Inefficiency, incompetence, and outright fraud are no strangers in the field of public administration, as illustrated in 1989 when the Department of Housing and Urban Development was engulfed by charges of waste, fraud, political favoritism, and conflict of interest. But even when bureaucracy works as planned, it still is an object of criticism and scorn.

Bureaucracies are strictly rule governed, which allows little space for innovation, stifles individuality, and fosters an impersonal quality in their dealings with the public. Rules require that everyone be treated the same, regardless of their particular problems and individual needs. Even if a person has a legitimate reason to expect special treatment, the bureaucrat's inevitable answer will be, "Sorry, those are the rules." As a result, bureaucracies are seen as aloof, unresponsive, and lacking accountability for their actions. People can be yelled at, reasoned with, persuaded, but rules are rules. Deviation from the regulations is a bureaucrat's most serious offense.

Because bureaucracies are creatures of habit, they are often slow in responding to sudden changes in the external political environment. If a new situation arises, requiring unprecedented action, a bureaucracy will tend to resort to a familiar, proven, but in the specific case, inappropriate, way of

*Employees of the Internal Revenue Service check tax returns. In order to operate efficiently, the federal government is organized into a bureaucracy—the work load is handled by specialized agencies, a hierarchy of authority controls the agencies, and the agencies adopt standard operating procedures.*

handling the problem. Further, bureaucracies are extremely protective of their own areas of operation. When an idea for a new program is put forth, bureaucrats may be more concerned with how it affects their budgets than whether it will be of value to the nation. When told of a proposal for a new federal program, President Kennedy responded, "That's a good idea. Now let's see if we can get the government to accept it." His remark was not meant in jest.

But despite the generally valid charges of inefficiency, impersonality, unresponsiveness, inertia, parochialism, and whatever else its critics come up with, the bureaucracy is not without its benefits. The enormous growth that has taken place in the federal government since the 1930s has been the direct result of the voters' demands for programs that meet real and often urgent needs. Social Security for the elderly, assistance for the poor and unemployed, financial aid for college students, regulations on the quality of food and medications, safeguards against fraudulent business practices, protections of

71

*Veterans wait in line to receive assistance at the Veterans Administration Medical Center in Washington, D.C. Because of the rules, paperwork, and time spent waiting in line, citizens often find dealing with agencies of the federal government frustrating and perplexing.*

workers' rights and job safety, and a host of other programs that benefit the majority of Americans are administered by that monster, "big government." Very few voters or politicians would favor dismantling the agencies that run these programs, and many people might say that the federal government should do even more in these areas. As long as the public demands services from the government, bureaucracy will continue to be a necessary evil.

## The Civil Service

Upon his inauguration in 1829, Andrew Jackson replaced a large number of presidential appointees and lesser officeholders with his own political supporters. A partisan senator defended this controversial action with the now-famous remark, "To the victor belong the spoils," and so the practice became known as the *spoils system*. The idea that a victorious politician has the right to reward followers with government jobs, however, did not originate with Jackson, but went back to the presidency of Thomas Jefferson. It was considered quite normal for workers from winning political campaigns to request rewards from the new officeholders whom they helped elect.

In the period just after the Civil War, the federal bureaucracy was rife with inefficiency and corruption, setting in motion a movement to reform the executive branch. Then, in July 1881 President James A. Garfield, an advocate of reform, was assassinated, just four months after his inauguration, by an office seeker who had been turned down for a government job. Chester A. Arthur, the new president, previously had opposed reform, but Garfield's murder and the ensuing public outcry changed his mind. With Arthur's backing, Congress passed the Civil Service Reform Act of 1883, establishing the modern *civil service system.*

Under the 1883 law, a bipartisan Civil Service Commission would fill federal jobs based on how applicants performed on competitive examinations. Originally, just 10 percent of all positions in the federal government were filled this way; today, 85 percent of the bureaucracy is covered by this merit-based system. Of the approximately 1 million jobs that are not part of the civil service system, many are in agencies that employ their own merit systems, such as

*An artist's sketch of the assassination of President James A. Garfield in 1881 by a mentally disturbed political supporter who had been denied a position in Garfield's administration. Garfield's death prompted passage of the Civil Service Act of 1883, which replaced the spoils system with the civil service system.*

*Applicants for clerical jobs in the State Department await their interviews. Under the civil service system, now administered by the Office of Personnel Management, jobs in the federal government are filled according to how applicants perform on competitive examinations.*

the U.S. Postal Service, the Federal Bureau of Investigation, and the Foreign Service.

The Civil Service Reform Act of 1978 replaced the Civil Service Commission with two agencies, the Office of Personnel Management (OPM) and the Merit System Protections Board. The OPM is the federal government's employment agency, handling applications and administering examinations for government jobs. When a position opens up, the OPM refers a list of eligible persons to the agency, which selects among the three top names on the list. The OPM also investigates the character of prospective government employees; however, if the job involves access to classified material, the FBI conducts a background check. The Merit System Protections Board protects civil servants from violations of merit rules, hears their appeals, and provides special protection for federal employees, so-called whistle-blowers, who report waste and corruption in their departments.

According to the Hatch Act (1939), federal civil servants may not take an active part in party politics nor run for political office. (They may, however, contribute to parties, attend rallies, wear campaign buttons, and display bumper stickers on their cars.) Although the Hatch Act has been challenged as an abridgment of federal employees' right of free speech, the Supreme Court upheld the act in *Civil Service Commission v. National Association of Letter Carriers* (1973). The Court ruled that the Hatch Act was created to prevent parties from exploiting federal workers in political campaigns and basing job promotions on party loyalty and, therefore, was consistent with the original intent of civil service reform—to remove the bureaucracy from the influence of politics.

# The Elements of the Federal Bureaucracy

More than 3.1 million people are employed by the federal government; of these, about 349,000, or 11 percent, work in the Washington, D.C., metropolitan area. As a means of comparison, in 1988 the largest American corporation, General Motors, had about 813,000 employees. More than a third of all federal workers are employed by a single agency, the Department of Defense. The federal bureaucracy is largely made up of three types of agencies: cabinet departments, independent executive agencies, and independent regulatory commissions.

## The Cabinet Departments

The 14 cabinet departments encompass about 60 percent of all federal employees and are directly responsible to the president. Each is headed by a presidential appointee, called a secretary (except for the Justice Department, which is run by the attorney general). Under the secretary is a deputy secretary and a number of assistant secretaries, each of whom is responsible for several offices in their respective departments.

Only three of the present cabinet departments existed during the administration of George Washington: the Departments of State, Treasury, and War (which in 1947 was consolidated with the Departments of the Navy and the Air Force and was renamed the Department of Defense in 1949). The Office of the Attorney General also dates back to 1789 and became the Department of Justice in 1870. Of the remaining 10 cabinet departments, the only one that was created during the nation's first 100 years is the Department of the Interior (1849).

The great expansion in the number of cabinet departments since the late 1800s reflects how industrialization created new issues and interest groups in America. For example, as a way of giving voice to the often conflicting concerns of farmers, businesses, and labor unions, Congress established the Departments of Agriculture (created in 1862), Commerce (1913), and Labor (1913). (Originally, in 1903, Commerce and Labor was a single department, presumably in the mistaken notion that workers and bosses share the same interests.) Departments such as Housing and Urban Development (1965), Transportation (1966), Energy (1977), and Health, Education and Welfare (established in 1953, but split in 1979 into the Department of Education and the Department of Health and Human Services) reflect the post–New Deal view that government can and should provide solutions to problems of modern, industrial society. The newest cabinet department is the Department of Veterans Affairs, which was created in 1989.

## Independent Executive Agencies

Although the numerous independent executive agencies resemble cabinet departments, they are not part of any such department. Like cabinet secre-

*President Ronald Reagan meets with his cabinet in November 1984. Each of the 14 cabinet departments is headed by a presidential appointee, who is confirmed by the Senate. All of the department heads (except the attorney general, who directs the Justice Department) are called secretaries.*

*Environmental Protection Agency technicians cover contaminated soil during one of their clean-up operations. The EPA, an independent executive agency, is responsible for protecting the nation's environment from pollution.*

taries, agency heads are appointed by and report directly to the president. Before 1989, in which year the interests of veterans were deemed worthy of cabinet status, the Veterans Administration had been the largest of these agencies. Other important independent executive agencies include the Central Intelligence Agency (CIA), the National Aeronautics and Space Agency (NASA), and the Environmental Protection Agency (EPA).

The National Archives and Records Administration, an independent executive agency, produces the *Federal Register*, a daily publication that informs federal agencies and the public of the rules and regulations of the executive branch. The *Federal Register* contains presidential proclamations and executive orders, as well as the current and proposed regulations and administrative orders of the federal agencies.

## Independent Regulatory Commissions

The independent regulatory commissions were created to establish rules and regulations for governing highly complex and technical fields that affect the public interest. For example, the Interstate Commerce Commission (ICC) regulates railroads, trucking companies, and bus lines; the Federal Trade Commission (FTC) prevents unfair competition, price fixing, and deceptive advertising; and the Federal Communications Commission (FCC) licenses radio and television stations and regulates the telecommunications industry.

These commissions are administratively independent of all three branches of the federal government. The president appoints their members—who must be drawn from both political parties—but cannot remove them. Although located within the executive branch, regulatory agencies perform legislative functions (when they make regulations), as well as judicial functions (when they prosecute and punish those who violate regulations). The regulatory commissions are, thus, a major exception to the constitutional principle of separation of powers.

Although administratively independent, the commissions are not free from political pressures. Regulatory commissions confer real benefits and costs, both on the industries being regulated and on the general public. As a result, presidents and members of Congress sometimes attempt to influence their actions by lobbying and mobilizing public opinion.

Moreover, regulatory commissions are subjected to pressures from the industries they regulate. Because decisions involving licenses, rate levels, and acceptable business practices affect profits, industries have a vested interest in trying to influence the members of a commission. Many political observers and members of Congress have argued that, in some cases, these agencies, instead of regulating industries in the public interest, have become their servants, some even might say, their captives. On the whole, however, the record of the last 100 years shows that these regulatory commissions have been generally beneficial to the public interest, curtailing the worst aspects of unregulated industry.

By the 1970s, government regulation of industry had become a target of widespread and often bipartisan criticism. President Jimmy Carter called for a cutback in regulation of the airline, banking, trucking, railroad, and telecommunications industries. When Ronald Reagan, who promised during his campaign "to take government off the backs of the people," became president in 1981, the trend accelerated.

By January 1985, the Civil Aeronautics Board, which set fares, granted air routes, and approved airline mergers, had been phased out of existence. Congress also reduced the powers of the ICC and the FTC. In 1987, the FCC abolished the fairness doctrine, which required broadcasters to present all sides of issues. But deregulation may have gone too far. For example, the

*United Airlines pilots walk the picket line at New York's La Guardia Airport in 1985. During the 1980s, the government's role in regulating many industries diminished. Many analysts believe that the deregulation of the commercial airlines led to the bankruptcies and labor strife that the industry experienced throughout the 1980s.*

airlines, since the early 1980s, have been riddled with financial losses, labor strife, layoffs, and numerous bankruptcies, for which many industry analysts and insiders blame the fare wars and unrestrained competition that resulted from deregulation.

## Government Corporations and Foundations

Government corporations, which are created and funded by Congress, provide important public services that are unprofitable for private companies to offer. Once a cabinet department, the U.S. Postal Service became a government corporation in 1970. Other government corporations include the Federal Savings and Loan Insurance Corporation, which protects savings bank deposits, and the Tennessee Valley Authority, which supplies electricity to all or parts of eight states.

Government foundations, such as the National Science Foundation and the National Foundation on the Arts and the Humanities, provide financial support for scientific research, the performing arts, and scholarship in the humanities.

# Bureaucratic Policy-making

The bureaucracy is, by definition, an apparatus of public servants who are responsible for carrying out the laws and policies made by elected officials, the president, and Congress. However, even the most casual student of modern American government will observe that it does far more than just this. In reality, the federal bureaucracy is a policy-making institution that initiates proposals, decides among various policy objectives and alternatives, and determines which interests will benefit from—or be harmed by—its actions.

In dealing with specific matters, bureaucrats often are free to select among alternative courses of action; thus, they have what is called discretionary power. And it is not just what a bureaucrat does that affects policy. Inaction, what a bureaucrat chooses not to do, is an equally important aspect of the policy-making process.

The bureaucracy's discretionary power is derived largely from the actions of Congress, an ironic situation because members of Congress have been known to bellow at length about the lack of accountability in bureaucratic decision making. The complex and technical nature of the issues that face an urban, industrialized society such as the United States—transportation, communications, economic growth and coordination, health care, and others—extend beyond the ability of Congress to make policy through legislation. Because most members of Congress are political generalists rather than specialists in such fields as science, engineering, or economics, they often find it necessary to delegate decision-making authority in a specific area to those who possess that specialized knowledge. Congress will draft a general statement of goals and propose actions for achieving these goals, but it will give the power to develop and execute specific policies to an agency in the bureaucracy (or, if no existing agency can handle the matter, it will create one).

Because bureaucratic agencies are acting on Congress's behalf, their decisions are just as binding as actual legislation—and they are more numerous. In an average year, Congress passes about 300 new laws, while the agencies issue around 7,000 new regulations. Thus, Congress has delegated to the bureaucracy a great portion of its constitutionally established legislative power.

The bureaucracy inevitably has become involved in politics because it is so heavily involved in making policy. Federal agencies, like elected officials, have their own constituencies—in their case, the interests that are regulated by the agency or affected by its decisions. These so-called client groups represent a crucial source of power that the bureaucracy is able to mobilize in its own

*The Federal Aviation Administration (FAA) holds a press briefing at its headquarters in Washington, D.C., following an airplane crash in July 1989. Congress has delegated much of its policy-making power to independent executive agencies and regulatory commissions. Government agencies issue approximately 7,000 new regulations annually.*

support. It is also politically important for an agency to have the support of Congress, especially the committee that oversees its operations and budget.

The term *iron triangle* refers to an alliance among an agency, a client group, and a congressional committee, in which all three parties benefit in some tangible way—the client group's interests are served, government programs or projects benefiting the home districts of the members of Congress are protected, and the agency's annual budget authorization increases at a healthy rate. The *military-industrial complex*, a term coined by President Eisenhower in his 1961 farewell speech, is a classic example of an iron triangle. Clearly, the military establishment, embodied in the Department of Defense, and the defense and aerospace industries both have a vested interest in pushing for increased military spending. These interests are promoted in Congress by members of the House and Senate Armed Services Committees, who tend to view the defense budget in terms of how it affects the military projects (bases,

81

*A Northrop Corporation technician checks a sophisticated guidance system used in the MX Peacekeeper missile system. Many observers argue that the military-industrial complex—the symbiotic relationship between the Department of Defense, the House and Senate armed services committees, and the defense industry—has worked to increase military spending beyond the level necessary to ensure the nation's defense.*

shipyards, defense contracts) that provide jobs for the voters in their districts. Other iron triangles consist of the subcommittees of the House and Senate agricultural committees that are concerned with specific farm products (such as cotton, tobacco, dairy products), the organizations that represent producers of particular agricultural commodities (the National Cotton Council, the Tobacco Institute, the Associated Milk Producers, for instance), and the agencies within the Agriculture Department that oversee programs concerning these commodities, such as the Agricultural Marketing Service and the Food Safety and Inspection Service.

Despite the existence of these iron triangles, the bureaucracy is frequently quite sensitive to public opinion. Agencies that enjoy the support of the American public can "cash in" that support for bigger budgets and increased autonomy. J. Edgar Hoover, who headed the FBI for four decades, took advantage of the Hollywood image of the FBI agent, or G-man, as a crime-fighting hero of almost mythic proportions. Hoover's bureau not only enjoyed annually increasing appropriations but also was able to engage in many questionable, and often illegal, activities without interference from politicians. Elected officials seldom are willing to risk the wrath of the voters by taking on agencies or programs that have wide public support. One needs only to consider the fate of any politician who might advocate the elimination of the Social Security program. On the other hand, an unpopular agency, such as the Internal Revenue Service, may be subjected to constant political criticism and investigations.

And so, bureaucracies invest much time and energy in creating a favorable image. Public relations is a normal part of business for many federal agencies. The 1960s would seem to have been a bad time to try to request billions of dollars for the exploration of space. Many Americans were clamoring for new national priorities, demanding that scarce fiscal resources be devoted to solving social problems. But with a masterful public relations campaign, NASA parlayed the country's fascination with space travel, and fears that the Soviets might accomplish it first, into the enormous budgetary outlays needed to land men on the moon—over and over again. NASA gave the nation its "Buck Rogers"; in return, Congress gave NASA its big bucks.

Early theorists in the field of public administration were influenced by the civil service reform movement and believed that politics and administration are distinct realms that should be kept separate. However, because the bureaucracy not only administers but also makes policy it is as much a political institution as Congress or the presidency. It has a constituency, it creates alliances with other policymakers, it is sensitive and responsive to public

*Astronaut Edwin "Buzz" Aldrin, the second person to walk on the surface of the moon, poses with the U.S. flag during the Apollo 11 mission. The National Aeronautics and Space Administration (NASA), the government agency responsible for space exploration, successfully convinced Congress to provide it with large budgets during the 1960s.*

, or circuits, each served by one of these courts. The
signed to each circuit ranges from 4 to 23; there are 186
ips. The decisions of the district courts, the independent
ons, and the United States Tax Court may be appealed in
ecisions are made by a panel of three judges; when there
e panel, it is resolved by a majority vote of all the judges
t, known as an *en banc* decision.
ated certain special courts to handle cases dealing with
eas of law. The Court of Military Appeals was established
appellate tribunal in court-martial convictions. Because
mposed of military officers, there is the danger that their
luenced by the views and interests of their commanding
son, this so-called G.I. Supreme Court is made up of three
are not subject to such pressures. The Court of Military
hat it handles criminal cases. The other special courts deal
lar aspects of federal civil law:

*stices in 1989. The Court, which contains nine justices*
*chief justice), has the power to decide cases of consti-*

opinion, and it even tries to shape public opinion to its advantage. In short, politics is a normal and necessary aspect of public administration.

# A "Fourth Branch" of Government?

Although it is located within the executive branch and, therefore, comes under the authority of the president, political scientists sometimes refer to the federal bureaucracy as a "fourth branch" of government—one that combines some of the functions of the three formally established branches. The bureaucracy arose and evolved in response to issues and problems of government that the writers of the Constitution could not have foreseen from their late-18th-century perspective. In so doing, it has built its own independent power base and developed its own set of vested interests. As modern presidents have lamented, the concerns of the bureaucracy and the White House are not always identical and an uncooperative bureaucracy can frustrate even the best intentioned of presidential initiatives. So whether or not the agencies of the federal bureaucracy constitute an additional branch of government, it is clear that, at the very least, they are a highly independent and extremely powerful force within the executive branch.

The U.S. Supreme Court building, located at 1 First St., N.E., in Washington, D.C. Article III of the Constitution established the Supreme Court as the highest court in the nation.

geographic districts
number of judges as
circuit court judgesh
regulatory commissi
the circuit courts. D
is a conflict among t
assigned to the cou

Congress has cre
specific issues and a
in 1950 as the final
military juries are co
decisions may be in
officers. For this rea
civilian judges, who
Appeals is unique in t
exclusively in particu

# Th

Article III of the Co
Supreme Court, but g
courts it decides are ne
of lower federal courts
these lower courts, cre
various special courts

## The Structu

The United States di
system. There are 94
District of Columbia, a
divided into as many a
are 575 district judg
citizens of different
(Disputes between ci
handled in state court

The United States
the federal judicial st

The Supreme Court j
(one of whom serves
tutional importance.

- The United States Tax Court handles tax cases.
- The United States Claims Court deals with claims for compensation against the government, tax refund cases, and claims of government employees for back pay.
- The United States Court of Appeals for the Federal Circuit hears copyright, trademark, and patent cases.
- The United States Court of International Trade decides cases involving federal taxes on imports, or tariffs.
- At the top level of the federal judiciary sits the Supreme Court, which is the highest court of appeal in the American system of justice. It can decide to uphold or overturn the rulings of lower federal courts and the highest courts of the 50 states. The Constitution did not set the number of Supreme Court judges, who are called "justices." Originally, there were 6, and throughout the 18th century the number ranged between 5 and 10, until in 1869, Congress fixed the number of Supreme Court justices at 9—8 associate justices and 1 chief justice.

# Judicial Selection and Appointment

Federal district and circuit court judges and Supreme Court justices are appointed by the president and must be confirmed by the Senate. No specific requirements for judicial appointees exist either in the Constitution or in law, but it is expected that they be lawyers. Judges are appointed "for good behavior," but because it is unusual, and difficult, for a federal judge to be impeached and removed from the bench, in practice this means a lifetime term. No Supreme Court justice has ever been impeached, although in 1969, Justice Abe Fortas, accused of conflict of interest and facing possible impeachment, resigned.

Despite the popular image of judges as impartial, objective defenders of the law—and so, removed from politics—the selection of federal judges is highly political and partisan. Indeed, presidents commonly use appointments to the federal bench to reward political allies for their help during the campaign. Thus, most judicial appointees are active members of the president's party. Gerald Ford nominated Republicans to fill 82 percent of the judicial vacancies during his administration, which was the lowest figure in this century. Woodrow Wilson appointed Democrats to 99 percent of the vacant judgeships during his tenure in office.

Presidents may subject potential nominees to a sort of ideological litmus test, making certain they agree with the administration's views on controversial issues. Franklin Roosevelt, for example, took care to nominate only judges who supported the philosophy and policies of his New Deal. Ronald Reagan gave preference to appointees who opposed past Supreme Court decisions legalizing abortion.

When a district judgeship in a particular state becomes vacant, the senator or senators from that state, if they belong to the president's party, submit a list of candidates to the president. (In the case of appeals courts, which encompass several states, senators informally divide up the judicial seats within the circuit.) The president selects one of these names, and the FBI conducts a background check on the nominee. The American Bar Association (ABA), the powerful interest group that represents the legal profession, evaluates the candidate's experience and qualifications and submits its own report; however, a president may ignore a negative ABA evaluation and make the nomination anyway.

Once the name is submitted to the Senate, the Judiciary Committee holds hearings in which the candidate is questioned and witnesses, both for and against, testify. The committee votes whether to recommend the nomination to the full Senate. If the committee gives its recommendation, the Senate votes to confirm or reject the nominee.

President Jimmy Carter worked to depoliticize judicial appointment, attempting to select federal judges, in his words, "strictly on the basis of merit without any consideration of political aspect or influence." Carter's efforts did have some impact; more women and minorities became federal judges during his administration than ever before. His successor, Ronald Reagan, reinstituted the Senate patronage system. More than 85 percent of Reagan's judicial appointees were white males, and 98 percent were Republicans.

Nominations to the Supreme Court tend to be even more politicized than district and circuit court selections. The ABA, interest groups, members of Congress, and even other Supreme Court justices have been known to lobby the president in the hope of influencing appointments to the high court. Chief Justice Warren Burger, for example, recommended that Nixon appoint Harry Blackmun, a friend since childhood, as an associate justice. The Supreme Court appointment of Sandra Day O'Connor was promoted both by the liberal National Organization of Women and her former law school classmate conservative justice (now chief justice) William Rehnquist.

Electoral considerations are also important. Presidents can appeal to minority groups in an especially conspicuous way by appointing one of their

*In June 1986, President Ronald Reagan announces the retirement of Chief Justice Warren Burger (far right) from the Supreme Court. Reagan introduces his new nominees for the Court: Associate Justice William Rehnquist (second from right) to succeed Burger as chief justice and Antonin Scalia (left) to succeed Lewis Powell as associate justice.*

members to the Supreme Court. The existence of so-called Catholic, black, and female seats on the Court is a political reality. (Until the late 1960s, there also was a "Jewish seat.") It is virtually certain that when the first black justice, Thurgood Marshall, leaves the bench, the incumbent president, Democrat or Republican, will find it politically wise to fill the vacancy with another black nominee. And as Hispanic voters become an increasingly influential and independent electoral bloc, it is likely that a Hispanic seat will be created on the Court.

Because the Supreme Court is such a powerful and visible institution, the Senate tends to scrutinize nominees very closely, particularly when the majority party is different from the president's party. Through 1989, the Senate, for various reasons, has failed to approve 27 of the 136 Supreme Court nominations (nearly 20 percent) that presidents have submitted. It rejected two of Nixon's appointees, one because of conflict of interest charges, the other because his record as an appeals court judge demonstrated both judicial mediocrity and racial bias. In 1987, the Senate rejected Reagan's nominee,

*Earl Warren, chief justice of the United States (1953–69). One of the first de-cisions that he wrote,* Brown v. Board of Education of Topeka, Kansas *(1954), set the stage for a long list of liberal decisions that distinguished the* Warren Court.

Federal Judge Robert H. Bork, because his controversial conservative views were perceived as too far from the judicial and political mainstream.

Appointing like-minded individuals to the Supreme Court is one of the most effective ways a president has of putting his political agenda into practice. Moreover, because Supreme Court appointments (and all federal judgeships) are virtually lifetime positions, a president can expect that at least some of his programs and policies will continue long after he has vacated the White House.

There is no guarantee, of course, that once confirmed, a justice will act in accordance with the president's wishes, or even his previous record. As attorney general and governor of California, Earl Warren built a record as a moderate Republican. In 1952, he supported his fellow Republican, Dwight D. Eisenhower, in his bid to win the party's nomination and then the presidency. But after Eisenhower appointed him chief justice, Warren took liberal positions on some of the most controversial issues of the postwar era—school desegregation, the rights of criminal defendants, and legislative reapportionment. Eisenhower came to regret his appointment of Warren, calling it "the biggest damn-fool mistake I ever made." Another Eisenhower appointee, Justice William Brennan, has remained one of the strongest liberal voices on the post-Warren Court of the 1970s and 1980s. For their part, liberal presidents have appointed their share of conservative justices. Justice James McReynolds, a Wilson appointee, was a notorious reactionary and archopponent of all moves for social or economic reform; Justice Byron White, a Kennedy appointee, has voted consistently with the Burger and Rehnquist conservative blocs. Nevertheless, when it comes to nominating federal judges, and particularly Supreme Court justices, political criteria are at least as important as merit. In other words, judicial selection is an inherently political process.

# How Cases Are Brought to the Supreme Court

Ten million cases are tried each year in the nation's courts. Of these, only about 5,000 are appealed to the Supreme Court, which then decides to hear arguments on fewer than 200. In short, most cases never get to the Supreme Court.

The cases that do reach the Court do so in one of three ways. By far the majority of cases that come under review by the Supreme Court do so because a litigant has filed a petition for a *writ of certiorari*, a legal term that is derived from the Latin word meaning "to inform or make certain." If four of the nine justices vote to grant the writ, the Court accepts jurisdiction in the case. In other words, it agrees to hear the case and directs the lower court to transmit to it the record of its proceedings in the case. The Court usually will grant certiorari only in cases that involve important constitutional questions. More than 90 percent of all applications for writs of certiorari are denied. Denial of certiorari is the most common type of Supreme Court action.

When the Supreme Court accepts jurisdiction by granting a writ of certiorari, it may schedule the case for oral argument, after which the justices vote to affirm or reverse the lower court's ruling. However, in cases where the issues are so clear that oral arguments would not change the mind of the individual justices, the Court may issue a summary decision. In this instance, the Court acts on the basis of the information in the certiorari briefs (the legal documents, pro and con, filed by the attorneys for the litigants in the case) and the record of the lower court proceedings. In other words, it reaches its decision without the benefit of oral argument.

Cases decided by lower federal or state courts that involve violations of constitutional rights may reach the Supreme Court under its appellate jurisdiction. In theory, at least, the Supreme Court is obliged to hear all such appeals. In practice, however, it can dismiss an appeal if it decides that no important constitutional issue is involved or make a summary decision without hearing oral arguments. Most summary decisions affirm the rulings of the lower courts. The Supreme Court, therefore, enjoys virtually unlimited discretion in the handling of appeals.

Finally, the Supreme Court has original jurisdiction in cases involving foreign diplomats or in which 1 of the 50 states is a party. It can hear such cases directly without their having to go through the process of either certiorari or appeal. However, the Court rarely exercises its power of original jurisdiction.


## "In the Opinion of the Court . . ."

The Supreme Court is in session from the first Monday in October usually through the end of the following June. During this period, the Court schedules oral arguments on the cases it has decided to hear. Each side gets half an hour to argue its position, and the process can be both lively and quite unnerving. The justices commonly interrupt, question, and engage in dialogue with lawyers who are presenting oral arguments before the Court.

On Fridays while the Supreme Court is in session, the justices meet in conference to discuss and vote on pending cases and certiorari petitions. The meetings are held in the strictest of privacy—one might even say, secrecy—

*A drawing that depicts the Supreme Court hearing oral arguments in* Regents of the University of California v. Bakke *in 1976. The Court held that a medical school's affirmative action program establishing strict racial preferences violated Title VI of the Civil Rights Act of 1964.*

with no one present except the nine justices. The chief justice chairs the conference and begins the discussion of each case, outlining what he feels the issues are and how they should be decided, before he casts his vote. The associate justices, in order of seniority, each give their views. These deliberations can become quite heated and take on a decidedly political character, as the justices debate their positions, form coalitions, attempt to persuade each other, and effect compromises. When the Court has come to a tentative decision on the case, the chief justice, if he is in the majority, assigns the task of writing the Court's opinion to one of the justices, or he may decide to do so himself. If he is in the minority, the most senior associate justice on the majority side assigns the writing of the opinion.

The opinion is a very important document. It explains why the majority of the Court voted as it did, outlining the relevant legal principles involved. It can establish a precedent that may influence how subsequent cases will be handled. Producing the opinion is an extremely time-consuming process. Drafts of the opinion are circulated among the justices for their comments. The other justices routinely suggest revisions and may change their votes when they see the final version of the opinion. For this reason, the justice who is assigned to write the Court's opinion tries to incorporate as broad a range of legal views as possible, not only to maintain the original majority, but also to win over members of the minority. Other justices may write dissenting opinions, if they disagree with the majority view, or concurring opinions, if they reached the same conclusion as the majority, but for different reasons.

Policymakers and interest groups generally feel that the existence of dissenting views tends to weaken the authority of a particular ruling. For this reason, the Court often places a high premium on unanimity, particularly when handling potentially divisive issues or precedent-setting decisions. To achieve

*Justice John Marshall Harlan (1877–1911) established a reputation as a liberal dissenter in civil rights cases. Harlan's dissenting opinion in* Plessy v. Ferguson *(1896), which severely criticized the majority's ruling that upheld segregated facilities for blacks, was vindicated by later Supreme Court decisions that struck down racially discriminatory laws and practices.*

a consensus, the chief justice may have to rely on the political arts of persuasion, bargaining, and even a bit of arm-twisting, as Chief Justice Earl Warren did in order to achieve the Court's unanimous ruling in the landmark 1954 case, *Brown v. the Board of Education of Topeka, Kansas*, in which the Court ruled that "separate, but equal" schools for blacks and whites were unconstitutional.

Over time, dissenting opinions may evolve into majority opinions. In 1896, Justice John Marshall Harlan vigorously attacked the Court's opinion that racial segregation may be permitted when there are "separate but equal" facilities for whites and blacks. His eloquent dissent—"our Constitution is color-blind, and neither knows nor tolerates classes among citizens"—formed the legal foundation of the Court's unanimous opinion in the *Brown* case 58 years later, when the doctrine of separate but equal was overturned.

Not until the opinion is completed does the Supreme Court announce its decision in a case. Usually at the beginning of each week that the Court is in session, new opinions are read or summarized in the courtroom, along with whatever dissenting or concurring opinions may have been written. At that time, the ruling finally is revealed and becomes law.

# Supreme Court Politics and Policy-making

Sitting at the pinnacle of the American judicial system, the Supreme Court is, obviously, the nation's top legal institution. It is, however, much more. The Court is equally a political institution, both in the way it reaches its decisions and in the impact that these decisions have on the nation as a whole. As much as any law passed by Congress or action taken by the president, its rulings affect, and sometimes alter, relationships between nation and state, government and business, and society and the individual. Interests can be either aided or hindered by its decisions. In short, the Supreme Court does more than merely interpret law—it also makes policy.

The Supreme Court is caught in a political tug-of-war. Conservatives look to it as a safeguard of property rights, privilege, and traditional values, while liberals expect it to protect civil rights and liberties and to act as a buffer against the worst abuses of uncontrolled business. Historically, most justices have identified more with conservative rather than liberal ideals. In general, the Court's political orientation remains stable for relatively long periods. For its first 150 years, for example, the Court staunchly championed the basic principle of *laissez-faire capitalism*—that government should not interfere in

The National Recovery Administration (NRA), lampooned in this cartoon, was the major component of Franklin Roosevelt's New Deal, a program designed to pull the country out of the Great Depression. The NRA was struck down in 1935 when the Supreme Court held that the agency was based on an act that constituted an unwarranted delegation of legislative powers to the executive branch.

the affairs of business. And its commitment to defending the civil rights of individuals is very much a contemporary trend.

The ideological shifts that the Supreme Court has undergone tend to reflect fundamental changes in the American political system. Thus, it was not until the end of the 1930s, by which time Franklin Roosevelt's New Deal programs were well established, that the majority of the Court began to take a more liberal view of government regulation of business, minority rights, and civil liberties. Over time, the Court's positions on these issues became at least as liberal as those of the other two branches, if not more so. But by the end of the 1980s, the Court, led by Chief Justice Rehnquist and packed with three Reagan appointees, began to abandon many of its previous liberal policies, reflecting the generally conservative shift in American politics.

The Supreme Court affects policy through *judicial review*, its power to declare laws or actions of federal and state executives unconstitutional and, therefore, invalid. The framers of the Constitution considered judicial review a fundamental and necessary power of the courts and included it in Article III. It was not firmly established in practice, however, until 1803. In his opinion in the case of *Marbury v. Madison*, Chief Justice John Marshall affirmed the principle that "a law repugnant to the Constitution is void, and the courts . . . are bound by that instrument." That is, the courts, and especially the Supreme Court, are obliged to strike down any law that violates the Constitution.

Today, judicial review is an established and generally accepted practice. Still, scholars, politicians, and the justices themselves disagree over to what extent the Supreme Court should exercise its power to rule on the actions of elected policymakers and, in effect, make policy itself.

One school of thought advocates *judicial restraint*, the idea that the Court should not initiate new policy departures but instead defer to the legislative branch. According to this view, justices generally should uphold acts of Congress unless they clearly violate a specific section of the Constitution. Above all, the Court should avoid so-called political questions that may lead it into conflict with the other branches of government, or worse, place it in the center of public controversy.

The opposing view, *judicial activism*, argues that because the Supreme Court is one of three constitutionally equal branches of the federal government, there is no reason that it should not join the president and Congress in making policy. In the 1950s and 1960s, for example, the Court, under Chief Justice Earl Warren, took the initiative on school desegregation, established protections for the rights of criminal defendants, and reapportioned legislatures to provide equal voter representation. These politically charged issues had been avoided by earlier Supreme Courts as well as by the other two branches of the government. In short, activist justices seek out ways of applying the Constitution to contemporary social and political questions.

Although they may appear so at first glance, judicial activism and judicial restraint are not synonymous with liberalism and conservatism, respectively. It is true that in the 1950s and 1960s, civil rights was the number one item on the liberal political agenda. By striking down the "separate but equal" principle, first in education, and later in general, the Warren Court steered a decidedly liberal course on this issue. In the mid-1930s, however, the Court was equally activist in overturning New Deal regulations on businesses. In that instance, the consequence of the Court's activism—the protection of business from government "interference"—was not liberal, but clearly conservative.

Similarly, in the late 1980s the Rehnquist Court went against precedent and began to chip away at existing civil rights and affirmative action policies, an activist course that nevertheless delighted conservatives and enraged liberals. Likewise, should it overturn the 1973 *Roe v. Wade* ruling legalizing abortion, the Court again will have employed the principle of judicial activism to achieve a conservative goal.

Judicial activism and judicial restraint, therefore, refer to whether the Supreme Court chooses to use the power of judicial review to affect policy in a significant way. They have nothing to do with the direction, liberal or conservative, that those policies take. That evaluation can be made only on a ruling-by-ruling basis.

Policymakers in the other branches of the government frequently feel that the initiatives of an activist Court are intrusive, that they overstep the judiciary's legitimate, constitutional bounds. Politicians often argue that justices should be strict constructionists. That is, they should apply the Constitution precisely as it was written, without adding anything to or inferring anything from the document. However, the Constitution is no more than a framework for government. The authors realized that government must be able to adapt to new issues and changing conditions, and so, the Constitution is intentionally flexible, even vague. The very existence of the elastic clause indicates that strict construction was the farthest thing from their mind.

The current controversy over original intent is of a similar nature. The idea that the justices should ascertain the intentions of the writers of the Constitution and employ these intentions as their guideline when making rulings is as questionable as the strict construction argument. Even if that were possible, it is hard to see why late-18th-century political ideas should be held up as authoritative in today's world. Further, as any historical account of the

In January 1980, thousands march down Pennsylvania Avenue in Washington, D.C., to voice their opposition to the Supreme Court's ruling in Roe v. Wade (1973), which legalized abortion. The Court's adoption of judicial activism or judicial restraint often affects the outcome of politically charged cases.

101

*Estelle Griswold (right), director of the New Haven Planned Parenthood League, waits outside a Connecticut court in 1962. In* Griswold v. Connecticut *(1965), the Supreme Court declared unconstitutional a state law prohibiting the use or distribution of birth control devices. The Court declared that the marital relationship was protected by a constitutional right to privacy listed in the Bill of Rights.*

Constitutional Convention makes clear, the delegates were far from unanimous in their views. The strict construction and original intent positions are not legal or judicial philosophies. Rather, they are political arguments that politicians and interest groups use to criticize an activist Supreme Court with whose decisions they disagree.

What the Supreme Court actually tries to do is discover the general meaning of the Constitution and apply it to concrete situations. For example, the Fourteenth Amendment, which provides for equal protection of the law for all citizens, does not refer to schools specifically, or even by implication. Nevertheless, in 1954 the Court interpreted it to mean that racial discrimination in public education was prohibited. Over time, the Court extended its interpretation of this portion of the Constitution to outlaw segregation in a wide range of situations and to protect the rights not only of blacks but also of women and other minorities.

Similarly, the Constitution, while enumerating many protected rights, nowhere mentions the right to privacy. Still, in a 1928 opinion, Justice Louis D. Brandeis—an advocate of judicial restraint, in fact—argued that the framers of the document certainly wanted to protect "the right to be let alone . . . the right most valued by civilized men," even if they did not say so. Brandeis found the right to privacy in the spirit, if not the words, of the Constitution.

Since then, the right to privacy has been protected not only by Supreme Court rulings but also by legislation. Its most controversial application occurred in the 1973 case of *Roe v. Wade,* when the Court ruled that the right to privacy includes the right to a legal abortion. This ruling, as the opinion stated, was based on the recognition "that a right of personal privacy . . . does exist under the Constitution," even though it does not enumerate this right explicitly.

Whether government may regulate business, whether school districts, landlords, or employers may discriminate on the basis of race or sex, whether women may obtain legal abortions—Supreme Court rulings have had an important, and often the most important, impact on these, and many other, questions of public policy. Thus, by interpreting the Constitution, the Supreme Court makes policy, and it does so with great discretion. After his retirement in 1941, Chief Justice Charles Evans Hughes admitted, "We are under a Constitution, but the Constitution is what the Supreme Court says it is."

*Pro-choice demonstrators rally at the Lincoln Memorial on the Mall in Washington, D.C., to urge lawmakers to keep abortions legal. People often join together to form interest groups such as pro-choice and pro-life organizations to influence government policy-making.*

# SIX

# Interest Groups and the Federal Government

When people join together on the basis of their common interests and try to influence policymakers to respond to these interests, they are said to belong to an *interest group*, or pressure group. It is understood that in a democracy, the people influence the government by voting in regularly scheduled elections. Interest groups, however, attempt to give people power beyond that of the voting booth. Individual voters combine their single votes into a political bloc by joining interest groups. The basic assumption is simple: in politics, there is strength in numbers. Interest groups also bridge the gaps between elections, thereby maintaining permanent pressure on policymakers. The idea here is that there should be no lull during which politicians can insulate themselves from the concerns of the voters. Interest groups, therefore, are designed as a means of exerting collective and continuous influence over the actions of government.

# Types of Interest Groups

There are as many types of interest groups as there are interests. The most powerful of these represent the major economic interests in American society—business, agriculture, and labor.

Businesses, large and small, desire a congenial economic environment in which to make their profits. Business interest groups want freedom from the "unnecessary interference" of government regulation in normal times and prompt assistance—such as the government's bailouts of Lockheed, Chrysler, and the savings and loan industry—in difficult ones. Small businesses have created their own organizations to help protect their unique interests, which at times may conflict with those of the larger enterprises. There also are numerous trade associations that represent specific industries and enterprises—such as banking, insurance, building, automotive, oil, and communications.

Agriculture also is a form of business; it is often referred to as "agribusiness." Agricultural interest groups look to the government to maintain farm commodity prices at a minimum level and to assist the farm economy during periods of natural disaster or economic crisis. As in the case of other businesses, the producers of the various agricultural commodities—beef, grain, dairy products, tobacco, and others—have created separate and powerful organizations to promote their distinct interests.

As a counterbalance to the power of big business, organized labor has established its own interest groups, the largest and most powerful of which is the American Federation of Labor and Congress of Industrial Organizations (AFL-CIO), a huge confederation which comprises the vast majority of the country's labor unions. Labor organizations attempt to influence government to protect the interests of working people in a wide range of areas—the right to unionize, health and safety on the job, unemployment compensation, minimum wage standards, and protection against plant closings. Fundamental changes in the economic and political conditions of the late 1970s and 1980s have decreased the power of labor somewhat, but it is still a formidable force in American politics.

Other types of interest groups focus more on social and political issues than strictly economic ones. Organizations such as the National Association for the Advancement of Colored People (NAACP), the National Organization for Women (NOW), and the American Association of Retired Persons (AARP), to name only three, respectively seek to protect the rights of blacks, women, the elderly, and other so-called minority groups in the society. Public interest

*The National Association for the Advancement of Colored People (NAACP) conducts a membership drive in the 1960s. The NAACP, an interest group concerned with social issues, lobbies for antidiscrimination laws.*

groups attempt to influence public policy in such areas as the environment, consumer affairs, energy, health care, and election reform. Examples of this type of interest group include Common Cause, a national citizen's lobby, and the numerous organizations associated with the noted consumer advocate Ralph Nader.

Finally, there are single-issue groups that are intensely and uncompromisingly committed to the attainment of a single policy goal. The classic example of this kind of interest group is the National Rifle Association (NRA), which vehemently opposes all attempts by the government to control or regulate firearms. In a similar vein, the National Right to Life Committee, formed just after the Supreme Court's 1973 *Roe v. Wade* ruling, is dedicated to banning abortions, by constitutional amendment, if necessary. On the other side of this issue, pro-choice groups such as the National Abortion Rights Action League (NARAL) are just as fervent about protecting women's rights to safe and legal abortions.

## How Interest Groups Influence Government

Interest groups attempt to influence policymakers through a variety of means. One way is by mobilizing their membership around a political goal. The NRA and Common Cause, for example, can marshal their supporters to deluge members of Congress, and even the president, with letters and phone calls on behalf of the group's position on a particular issue. The sheer volume of mail that an official receives is an important consideration; some political observers believe that politicians at least count their mail, even it they do not read it.

Interest groups also try to build a positive image and create a favorable climate for their political goals by molding public opinion. In recent years, the NRA, the National Right to Life Committee, and the AFL-CIO have hired public relations firms to create aggressive and expensive direct mail and media advertising campaigns through which they hope to convince a large percentage of the general population of the validity of their views. When interest groups can appeal successfully to a significant portion of the voters, politicians find it difficult to ignore their demands or dismiss them as narrow and unrepresentative. Mass propaganda is a basic political tool for interest groups.

Events such as public rallies and mass demonstrations are important ways of attracting media attention to, and mobilizing large-scale support for, a particular cause. This is especially crucial for less affluent groups with limited resources who cannot afford major public relations campaigns. Large demonstrations—

*National Rifle Association (NRA) president Brigadier General Joe Foss speaks to the National Press Club in 1989. Foss blasted those people urging controls on the sale of military-style assault rifles, asserting that the criminal element and not the weapon should be controlled. NRA lobbyists attempt to persuade Congress to reject major gun-control bills.*

such as the 1963 March on Washington, in which more than 200,000 people, black and white, converged on the capital to demand civil rights reforms—were extremely important in convincing politicians of the level of commitment and grass roots strength of the civil rights movement. Militant protests throughout the late 1960s and early 1970s ultimately turned the tide of domestic sentiment against the war in Vietnam, especially when many returning veterans joined the antiwar movement. Since 1973, the National Right to Life Committee has staged demonstrations in Washington to voice its opposition to abortion. In the late 1980s, as abortion rights began to come under increasing attack, pro-choice groups such as NOW and NARAL organized mass demonstrations on behalf of the right to legal abortion.

Many interest groups also rely on a more direct approach—*lobbying*. Representatives of interest groups attempt to engage in direct communication with policymakers—in Congress, the White House, the bureaucracy, and even the courts—in order to influence their decisions. Large professional, trade, and political associations (such as the American Medical Association, the American

*Labor lobbyists meet at AFL-CIO headquarters in Washington, D.C., to coordinate their efforts on Capitol Hill. By establishing friendships with lawmakers, lobbyists are able to present the views of the interest groups that they represent.*

Farm Bureau Federation, and the AFL-CIO) usually have their own in-house lobbyists. Corporations may employ high-priced Washington law firms to represent them; these firms can offer inside knowledge of how the system works, and more important, access to a wide network of friends and contacts in government. Public relations and consulting firms, often set up by former government employees, also represent interest groups as lobbyists.

For the successful lobbyist, personal contact is essential. Lobbyists believe that the best way to influence policy is to cultivate friendships with key government officials or their staffs. In this way, when an issue of concern arises, there is a ready avenue through which the lobbyist can present the position of his or her group to the policymaker.

The personal contacts that lobbyists make with members of Congress and their staffs can be equally beneficial to those in government. It is not unusual, for example, for a staff member of the House Agricultural Committee to get a job as a lobbyist for the cotton or beef industry or for a Senate Armed Forces Committee staff member to be hired by a defense contractor. Federal law now prohibits former employees of the executive branch from appearing before their old departments or agencies to represent clients for at least one year after leaving government service. Nevertheless, when that period has expired, ex-members of the executive branch often become lobbyists for private interests with which they once had dealings.

Moreover, federal employees, by law, may not use their positions to profit themselves or a future employer. Nevertheless, a survey of former Defense Department employees who later worked for defense contractors found that, while still at the Pentagon, one-quarter of these ex-bureaucrats had been in a position to affect the interests of their future employer. In addition, 20 percent of them eventually worked on projects that they previously had overseen. Such findings as these tend to support the views of many political observers who argue that the close relationships between lobbyists and government officials have become a breeding ground for conflict of interest and influence peddling.

In presenting their case to government officials, lobbyists generally adhere to a set of informal guidelines. Honesty is important. Lobbyists who claim that their position is in the public interest make little impression on most policymakers. Legislators and bureaucrats are not that easily fooled; they realize that lobbyists are political animals who speak for particular interests. Moreover, policymakers feel that they can decide for themselves what is in the public interest. What they want is a clear presentation of the lobbyist's position and information on which to base their ultimate decision. Lobbyists who do solid, reliable research, such as Ralph Nader's various consumer organizations, can influence public policy because government officials often depend heavily upon them.

Lobbyists must understand how to play the game of politics. Effective lobbyists do not threaten, bluff, or ask for too much too often. They must be willing to compromise, because opposing interests have staked their own claim on the attention of policymakers. A lobbyist who demands everything may end up with nothing.

Without a doubt, the lobbyist's most powerful tool is money. Of course, direct bribes to government officials are illegal. They are also unnecessary. Lobbyists for interest groups can use money to influence public officials in a perfectly legal way—through campaign contributions and fund-raising. For example, after the dairy industry contributed $2 million to Richard Nixon's reelection campaign in 1972, there was an increase in milk price supports worth more than $300 million to milk producers—a most profitable "investment." The American Medical Association routinely contributes money to elect legislators who are opposed to national health insurance and federal regulation of health care costs. And the AFL-CIO's political arm, the Committee on

111

*Consumer advocate Ralph Nader holds a news conference in 1988 to publicize a report on the decline of quality in Cadillac automobiles. Reputable lobbyists such as Nader can influence public policy because lawmakers respect their opinions.*

Political Education (COPE), not only contributes money and endorses candidates, as do most interest groups, but also runs voter registration drives and provides campaign volunteers for the politicians it supports.

Perhaps the most significant development in American politics in the 1980s was the emergence and proliferation of *political action committees* (PACs). In 1974 there were around 600 PACs; by 1990 there were nearly 4,200. Interest groups establish PACs to further their policy goals by channeling money to elect—and sometimes defeat—particular candidates for political office. For example, in 1980, the National Conservative Political Action Committee (NCPAC) launched an intensive and expensive effort to unseat five so-called superliberal senators; four of these incumbents were defeated in the November elections.

Although federal law limits the amount of money that an individual or group can contribute to the campaign of a particular candidate, in 1975 the Supreme

*Roger Viguerie, a businessman and political activist, supports several conservative interest groups. Viguerie is noted for his ability to raise funds for interests groups through direct-mail campaigns.*

Court held that restrictions on "independent expenditures" made on behalf of candidates, but without their cooperation, were unconstitutional. Thus, the amount that PACs can contribute *directly* to a candidate's campaign may be limited by law, but, because PACs are formally independent organizations, they may spend an unlimited amount of money that *indirectly* benefits the candidate. It is not unusual during a political campaign to see television ads in support of a candidate that were not produced and paid for out of the candidate's campaign fund. These ads were paid for by PACs.

PAC contributions are designed to maintain and strengthen the group's influence within Congress. If there is a political truism in Washington today, it is that winning a seat in the House is the same as getting a lifetime job. A large part of the reason is that special interests, through their PACs, contribute big money to reelect incumbents. In the 1988 campaign, 79.1 percent of PAC money went to incumbents and only 11.7 percent to challengers (with 9.2 percent spent in races where there was no incumbent candidate.) In Senate races, 68.3 percent of PAC money went to incumbents, itself an overwhelming proportion.

Incumbency naturally carries with it a number of built-in advantages when reelection time rolls around. For example, incumbents are better known by the voters than are their opponents; they can carry out favors for constituents (such as cutting bureaucratic red tape); and they have access to free-mail privileges, known as "franking." (Political consultants estimate that the frank is worth at least $350,000 in campaign funds.) Still, in the 1988 elections, 98.3 percent of House incumbents were returned to Washington, which exceeded the 20-year average of 94 percent and a testament of the power of interest groups and their PACs to influence government.

# The Pluralist Model of Government

Among political scientists, the prevailing theory of how government makes policy is called *pluralism*. Pluralism is said to exist when many interests have access to the government and compete with each other to influence policy decisions. The basic unit of the pluralist model, therefore, is the interest group. One of the earliest and most influential presentations of pluralism was Robert A. Dahl's *Who Governs?*, a study of power and decision making in New Haven, Connecticut, in the late 1950s. Dahl's conclusions were generalized and

*In November 1988, more than 300 members of ACT NOW, a group promoting public awareness of issues concerning AIDS (acquired immune deficiency syndrome), demonstrate in front of the U.S. Department of Health and Human Services building in Washington, D.C., to protest the Reagan administration's handling of the AIDS epidemic. According to the pluralist model, government is successful because many interest groups compete with each other to influence government policy decisions.*

applied to all levels of government in the United States: local, state, and federal.

Pluralist theory attempts to reconcile the ideals of democracy, in particular the notion of full and open participation by the citizenry in their government, with the indisputable fact that in the United States most people do not actively participate in politics. The central assumption is that because enough people belong to enough interest groups, the government, in effect, hears everyone. Government, then, is viewed as an arena in which groups compete and compromise for influence over policy, but where no single interest can dominate.

Pluralism is widely, but not universally, accepted among students of American government. As an alternative to the pluralist model, sociologist C. Wright Mills developed what is known as *elite theory*. In his 1956 book, *The*

*Workers prepare a shipment of guidance systems for Sparrow missiles, which are used by the U.S. Air Force. Some political observers assert that the political influence of powerful coalitions such as the military-industrial complex casts doubt on the ability of the federal government to meet the needs and concerns of the public.*

*Power Elite*, he argued that in America, crucial decisions concerning economic and foreign policy are made by a small, exclusive cadre of top business executives, military leaders, and the highest officials of the executive branch. In other words, according to Mills, power over issues of war and peace, and boom and bust, is exercised by an economic, military, and political elite—the few, not the many.

Other scholars, who have been influenced, to at least some extent, by Mills's theory, have raised some concrete criticisms of the pluralist version of how government works. Political scientist Theodore J. Lowi has questioned whether the pluralist notion of government by interest groups is really as desirable as its advocates claim. He has argued that the influence of these groups and their narrow interests severely limits the ability of government to address new social problems and political issues as they arise and to make policy in the public interest. For example, pressure from agricultural groups to maintain minimum prices on farm commodities hampers the government's ability to fight inflation, even though lower food prices would be in the interest of the public. Such a government is, according to Lowi, impotent and inherently unjust.

Some political scientists maintain that pluralism does not guarantee democratic openness. The pluralist model considers only decisions that are made by government. But what about issues that never reach the political agenda? For example, political scientist Matthew A. Crenson demonstrated that in Gary, Indiana, United States Steel Corporation inhibited even the discussion of local air pollution controls. Pollution became a "non-issue," not subject to the competition and bargaining that the pluralist theorists praise. When powerful interests can prevent an issue from being raised, pluralism has failed.

Further, some political observers question whether pluralism really exists in practice to any significant extent. The existence of "iron triangles"—cozy and mutually beneficial alliances that powerful interests establish with sectors of the bureaucracy and Congress—casts doubt on the openness of government and its ability to respond to the concerns of the public. In particular, the close relationship between the defense and aerospace industries and the military establishment stands as a compelling counterexample to the assumptions of the pluralist model.

In 1961, President Eisenhower, a former general, cautioned that the American people must take care to prevent this military-industrial complex from gaining unwarranted influence over the government. In the decades since Eisenhower's solemn warning, the power of the military-industrial complex has grown enormously, as illustrated by the huge and annually increasing level of defense contracts. In fiscal 1987, federal defense contracts totaled $142 billion; more than 10 percent of that figure went to just 2 recipients, McDonnell Douglas and General Dynamics.

Finally, there are two demographic factors that undermine the validity of pluralism: First, less than one-third of the population belong to interest groups; second, those who do tend to be better educated and come from the higher income levels. The poor are less well organized and generally lack the financial resources that would enable them to compete in the political arena on equal terms with people of higher social and economic status. In practice, interest group politics is less representative of the population as a whole and more biased in favor of business interests and the affluent than pluralist theory claims.

117

*George Bush celebrates his victory in the 1988 presidential elections with a crowd of supporters.*

# SEVEN

# Federalism in the United States

$A$ system of government in which all power is vested in a single central government is known as a *unitary system*. Under such a system, the national government may create subnational governments and grant them whatever powers it sees fit. These subnational units, then, are dependent on the national government that gave them their authority and that also may revoke it. Examples of unitary governments include Great Britain, France, and Israel.

The United States, on the other hand, is governed by a *federal system*. In such a system, power is divided between the national government and various subnational governments, such as the 50 states. The states are, of course, subject to the laws made by the national government. Unlike a unitary system, however, they are not the creations of the central government; in a federal system, the authority of the states is constitutionally independent of the national government. Canada, West Germany, Switzerland, and the Soviet Union also are governed by federal systems.

## The Foundations of American Federalism

In the United States, federalism existed even before the Constitution. The original political structure of the new nation, the Articles of Confederation,

119

*James Madison, the chief architect of the U.S. Constitution, advocated a strong central government with an independent federal court system, a strong executive, and a bicameral legislature.*

created a system in which the governments of the 13 separate states had much more power than the skeletal national government. It quickly became apparent, however, that this was an inherently weak form of government, prone to disunity and instability.

The Constitution attempted to correct the worst flaws of the Articles of Confederation, while maintaining its overall federalist character. Even before the Constitutional Convention, James Madison realized that a single central government would be politically unattainable. He observed that despite the failure of the Confederation, the popular sentiment in the United States was suspicious of the idea of a strong central government and held onto federalist notions. Loyalty to the states was steadfast; the revolutionary war, it must be remembered, was fought in large part by an alliance of state militias. And of course, the war itself was a struggle for independence from the suffocating power of a strong central government, the British monarchy. Madison knew that the advocates of a strong national government would have to compromise with the supporters of federalism, who wanted to curb the concentrated power of the central government. So, as he wrote to George Washington, Madison decided to seek "a middle ground which may at once support a due supremacy of the national authority, and not exclude the local authorities."

In the end, the Constitution established a strong national government but preserved the authority of the state governments. It prohibited the states from exercising certain powers, such as coining money or declaring war on a foreign nation, but also limited the powers of the national government, in particular, denying it the power to change state boundaries or create new states out of existing states. (Because local governments derive their authority from the states of which they are a part, they are subject to the same constitutional limitations as the states.) The essential principle of American federalism is expressed in Article VI, Paragraph 2, the so-called supremacy clause, which states that the Constitution and the laws that Congress makes under it are supreme over state constitutions and laws. Whenever there is a conflict between state and federal law, federal law must prevail.

Article IV, Section 4, defines the federal government's obligations to the states. It must guarantee a republican form of government to every state, in which the people vote for their representatives and rights are guaranteed by a constitution. The federal government also must protect the states from both foreign invasion and domestic violence. Although the federal government is supposed to intervene at the request of the governor or legislature of the particular state, on certain occasions presidents have sent troops to restore order in states against the wishes of state authorities. During the civil rights

121

*A Birmingham, Alabama, policeman uses an attack dog against an unarmed civil rights demonstrator in 1963. Although the Constitution provides that the federal government may intervene to protect the states from domestic violence only at the request of the states, President John F. Kennedy sent federal troops into southern states without the consent of the states during the civil rights struggles of the 1960s.*

struggles of the 1960s, for example, uninvited federal troops protected demonstrators against violence perpetrated by the local citizenry, as well as the local police, in many southern states. Southern governors railed long and loud against such federal "interference."

The Tenth Amendment, ratified with the Bill of Rights in 1791, sought to clarify the relationship between the federal and state governments. It says simply that any powers not delegated to the federal government by the Constitution nor prohibited by it, are reserved to the states. However, the Supreme Court's ruling that Article I, Section 8, the elastic clause, gives Congress a broad range of implied powers not specifically stated in the Constitution, rendered the Tenth Amendment virtually insignificant in practice.

The Constitution established a federalist system of government in the United States, striking a delicate balance between the power of the national government and the rights of the states. But despite the supremacy and elastic clauses, the key question of who should have the ultimate political authority, the national government or the separate states, was, in practice, still unclear. Over time, the powers of the different levels of government began to overlap in many areas, a situation which could, and did, lead to internal disharmony, political conflict, and worse.

Although slavery was the specific issue that brought the matter to a head, the Civil War was essentially a dispute over a fundamental problem of federalism—whether the federal government or the states should be the dominant political voice. Advocates of states' rights argued that the Constitution was a union created by the states—note the name, "United States"—which granted limited powers to the federal government. According to this view, if the federal government attempted to go beyond its narrow, constitutional authority, the states would be justified in defying it and, if necessary, seceding from it. Those who supported a strong central government, however, maintained that because the Constitution had been ratified by the people, the national government was the highest authority, not the states. After 5 years of war and 500,000 fatalities, the latter view prevailed, and the Union was preserved.

# Federalism in the 20th Century

From the 19th century until the late 1930s, American federalism was characterized by a tenuous balance between the powers of the federal and state governments. The outcome of the Civil War reaffirmed the notion of a strong

# CHARLESTON

# MERCURY

## EXTRA:

Passed unanimously at 1.15 o'clock, P. M. December 20th, 1860.

### AN ORDINANCE

*To dissolve the Union between the State of South Carolina and other States united with her under the compact entitled "The Constitution of the United States of America."*

We, the People of the State of South Carolina, in Convention assembled, do declare and ordain, and it is hereby declared and ordained,

That the Ordinance adopted by us in Convention, on the twenty-third day of May, in the year of our Lord one thousand seven hundred and eighty-eight, whereby the Constitution of the United States of America was ratified, and also, all Acts and parts of Acts of the General Assembly of this State, ratifying amendments of the said Constitution, are hereby repealed; and that the union now subsisting between South Carolina and other States, under the name of "The United States of America," is hereby dissolved.

# THE

# UNION

## IS

# DISSOLVED!

*A special edition of the Charleston* Mercury *announces South Carolina's secession from the United States on December 20, 1860, and underscores the inevitability of the Civil War. The dispute over whether the federal government or the states should be the dominant political force was one of the major disagreements that led to the Civil War.*

124

central government, but competition and conflict between the levels of government nevertheless continued. Frequently the Supreme Court had to be called in to referee the dispute. National and state governments were viewed as both distinct and equal, at least in the sense that each was supreme in its own area. This concept, known as *dual federalism*, reflected the political circumstances of the post–Civil War era, an uneasy equilibrium between the fundamental authority of the national government and the still formidable power of the separate states.

In the wake of the Great Depression of the 1930s, Franklin Roosevelt's New Deal initiated a broad range of federal social welfare and public works programs. The country's economy stood on the brink of collapse; it was a national crisis that could be addressed only by a national solution. As a result of the New Deal, the power of the federal government expanded beyond that of the states. Once the Supreme Court, in 1937, began to recognize these programs as constitutional, the era of *cooperative federalism* was launched.

According to this concept, the national and state governments are components of a governing system in which powers are shared and responsibilities carried out jointly. The distribution of payments to farmers, the provision of social services, and the planning and building of the interstate highway system are examples of how the federal and state governments work together to carry out ambitious tasks and handle large-scale problems. But even though the functions and powers of government are shared between the different levels, the control center of the system is Washington, D.C. There, tax revenues are collected from the states and then redistributed back to them in the form of federal financial aid. Through its constitutional powers of taxation and appropriation, the national government can exert control over the fiscal resources of the states. As a result, it has emerged as the dominant element in the American federalist system.

For fiscal year 1989, the level of federal aid to state and local governments represented about 11 percent of the federal budget, approximately $120 billion. To receive federal aid, state and local governments usually have to meet matching requirements. That is, they must put up some of their own money in order to receive federal dollars. According to a formula that takes into account fiscal strength or weakness, poor states pay less than rich ones.

 Federal aid to states and localities comes in three forms. The largest amount of federal money (88 percent) consists of categorical grants (or grants-in-aid), funds that are designated to be used for specific purposes, such as pollution control or bridge and highway repair. Block grants (11 percent), which may be used for a range of purposes within a broad area such as education or

*The interchange of Interstates 40 and 65 in Davidson County, Tennessee. The construction of the interstate highway system is an example of how the federal and state governments work together to carry out shared responsibilities.*

community development, and general purpose grants (1 percent), which may be spent by the recipients for whatever purposes they wish, account for the rest. In fiscal 1989, more than 56 percent of the total federal money received by states and localities was allocated for the areas of health, welfare, and income security, with most of that funding going for welfare and medical assistance programs.

Federal expansion is an accomplished fact. Still, opponents of this trend may attempt to rally public sentiment and stimulate political action by resurrecting 19th-century federalist ideas. In 1948, many southern Democrats were upset when, at the national convention, a civil rights plank was inserted into the party platform. In protest, they bolted from the convention hall and ran Senator Strom Thurmond as the presidential candidate of the splinter States' Rights, or Dixiecrat, party. (Thurmond received only 2.4 percent of the popular vote.) For the next two decades, the *states' rights* concept served as a pretext to perpetuate segregation. Defenders of states' rights viewed civil rights legislation as gross interference by the federal government, an illegitimate infringement on states' rights. In the mid-20th century, just as in the pre–Civil War era, the cause of states' rights was invoked by those who wanted to preserve the power and privilege of whites, as well as the oppression of blacks, in the South.

In the 1980s, Ronald Reagan's New Federalism again showed how federalist ideas have been used to promote a conservative agenda. In his first inaugural address, Reagan outlined his personal vision of federalism:

> It is my intention to curb the size and influence of the federal establishment and to demand recognition of the distinction between the powers granted to the federal government and those reserved to the states or to the people. All of us need to be reminded that . . . the states created the federal government.

Over the next year or so, under the heading of New Federalism, he proposed a major restructuring of the relationship between federal and state governments, including transferring many joint programs such as welfare and food stamps completely to the states. (In its original use, during the Nixon administration, "new federalism," stood for more control by the states and localities over how federal aid was spent; it did not mean a smaller role for the federal government.) The fundamental idea behind Reagan's New Federalism was that states and localities should spend only what they can raise on their own.

127

*In the historic setting of the Capitol's Rotunda, President Ronald Reagan delivers his inaugural address in January 1985 after being sworn in for his second term of office. Reagan attempted to reduce the size and influence of the federal government; however, Congress opposed his plan to restructure the relationship between federal and state governments.*

State governors and city mayors complained that they did not have the fiscal resources to pay for the programs that Reagan wanted to dump on them. Critics argued that this New Federalism was merely a bid to dismantle the New Deal, a thinly veiled attempt to eliminate many of the social welfare programs that, for decades, conservatives abhorred. During the Reagan years, federal grants were reduced by more than 4 percent, some categorical grants were eliminated, and other programs were consolidated into block grants. Still, Congress rejected the president's ambitious restructuring scheme, and so, the overall structure of federal-state relations remains essentially unaltered.

# The Debate over Federalism

Advocates of federalism claim that it offers a number of benefits over a unitary system of government. For instance, it is assumed that local governments can handle local issues more efficiently and effectively than a far-off national bureaucracy. Each locality has its own unique circumstances, and a federal system would ensure that public policy will be tailor-made to fit specific, local conditions.

In a federal system, it is argued, government is closer to the people. Because there are more levels of government, there are more access points through which citizens can influence policymakers to act in the public interest. As a result, the level of political participation in the society should increase and greater democracy be achieved.

A federal system, in which political power is decentralized and diffused, is thought to be a better protector of individual rights than a more centralized system, where political power is concentrated. Finally, federalism reinforces and preserves the abundant geographic, ethnic, and racial diversity that characterizes the population of a country like the United States. So go the major arguments on behalf of a federal system.

Critics of federalism, however, feel that they can counter each of these apparent benefits. It is all well and good to claim that local governments best understand local issues, but they may lack the expertise and, even more important, the money to adequately address these concerns. Moreover, local problems usually are manifestations of national issues; a proliferation of piecemeal local solutions can complicate the creation of a coherent national policy.

What about the notion that a government that is closer to the people and characterized by many access points is necessarily more responsive to the public interest and more democratic? In reality, such a government does not guarantee political openness. The power wielded by the coal industry in West Virginia, the oil industry in Texas, the tobacco industry in North Carolina, or a single corporation, Du Pont, in Delaware, would indicate that state and local governments are even more susceptible than the national government to the influence of special interests.

Historically, the critics of federalism say, it was through state and local governments that southern segregationists attempted to thwart the civil rights reforms that, in fact, originated at the national level. Federalism, embodied in the call to defend states' rights, worked to protect privilege and discrimination, not individual liberties. Finally, it may not be entirely desirable to encourage

*Kathleen Kennedy Townsend, a Democratic candidate for Maryland's second congressional district seat, leaves the voting booth accompanied by her family. Ultimately, voters influence government policies at the ballot box by supporting or rejecting legislators.*

130

*On September 17, 1987, crowds gather at Independence Hall in Philadelphia to hear a bell ringing, which commemorated the signing of the Constitution on the same date in 1787. The Constitution, which remains the foundation of the federal government, was honored throughout the country during celebrations of its bicentennial.*

and preserve diversity within the population, for diversity can lead to divisiveness and political disunity. Rather, national governments need to create the sense of a common, national identity among the citizenry.

The compromise that the authors of the Constitution struck between a stable central government and the continued authority of the states has evolved into a federal system characterized by complexity and contradictions. Over time, the power of the national government came to surpass that of the states. Yet, Americans continue to cling to the ideas of local control and political decentralization. And despite the growth of federal power, the state governments did not wither away, but expanded, as well. In short, all levels of government—federal, state, and local—are far more powerful today than they were when the ineffective Articles of Confederation were superseded by a bold experiment in government, the Constitution of the United States.

131

# Appendix:
# Government Agencies

## *Legislative Branch*

Architect of the Capitol
United States Botanic Garden
General Accounting Office
Government Printing Office
Library of Congress
Office of Technology Assessment
Congressional Budget Office
Copyright Royalty Tribunal
United States Tax Court

## *Judicial Branch*

United States Courts of Appeal
United States District Courts
United States Claims Court
United States Court of Appeals for the Federal Circuit
United States Court of International Trade
Territorial Courts
United States Court of Military Appeals
Administrative Office of the United States Courts
Federal Judicial Center

## *Executive Office of the President*

White House Office
Office of Management and Budget
Council of Economic Advisors
National Security Council
Office of Policy Development
Office of the United States Trade Representative
Council on Environmental Quality
Office of Science and Technology Policy
Office of Administration

## Independent Establishments and Government Corporations

ACTION

Administration Conference of the U.S.

African Development Foundation

American Battle Monuments Commission

Appalachian Regional Commission

Board for International Broadcasting

Central Intelligence Agency

Commission on the Bicentennial of the United States Constitution

Commission on Civil Rights

Commission of Fine Arts

Commodity Futures Trading Commission

Consumer Product Safety Commission

Environmental Protection Agency

Equal Employment Opportunity Commission

Export-Import Bank of the U.S.

Farm Credit Administration

Federal Communications Commission

Federal Deposit Insurance Corporation

Federal Election Commission

Federal Emergency Management Agency

Federal Home Loan Bank Board

Federal Labor Relations Authority

Federal Maritime Commission

Federal Mediation and Conciliation Service

Federal Reserve System, Board of Governors of the

Federal Retirement Thrift Investment Board

General Services Administration

Inter-American Foundation

Interstate Commerce Commission

Merit Systems Protection Board

National Aeronautics and Space Administration

National Archives and Records Administration

National Capital Planning Commission

National Credit Union Administration

National Foundation on the Arts and the Humanities

National Labor Relations Board

National Mediation Board

National Science Foundation

National Transportation Safety Board

Nuclear Regulatory Commission

Occupational Safety and Health Review Commission

Office of Personnel Management

Panama Canal Commission

Peace Corps

Pennsylvania Avenue Development Corporation

Pension Benefit Guaranty Corporation

Postal Rate Commission

Railroad Retirement Board

Securities and Exchange Commission

Selective Service System

Small Business Administration

Tennessee Valley Authority

U.S. Arms Control and Disarmament Agency

U.S. Information Agency

U.S. International Development Cooperation Agency

U.S. International Trade Commission

U.S. Postal Service

# The Government of the United States

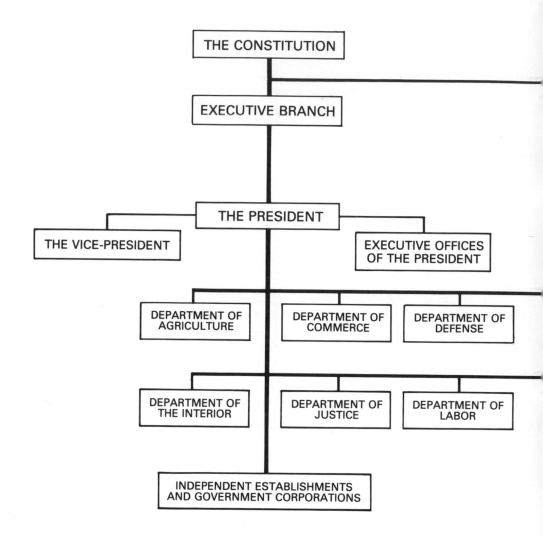

THE CONSTITUTION

EXECUTIVE BRANCH

THE PRESIDENT

THE VICE-PRESIDENT

EXECUTIVE OFFICES OF THE PRESIDENT

DEPARTMENT OF AGRICULTURE

DEPARTMENT OF COMMERCE

DEPARTMENT OF DEFENSE

DEPARTMENT OF THE INTERIOR

DEPARTMENT OF JUSTICE

DEPARTMENT OF LABOR

INDEPENDENT ESTABLISHMENTS AND GOVERNMENT CORPORATIONS

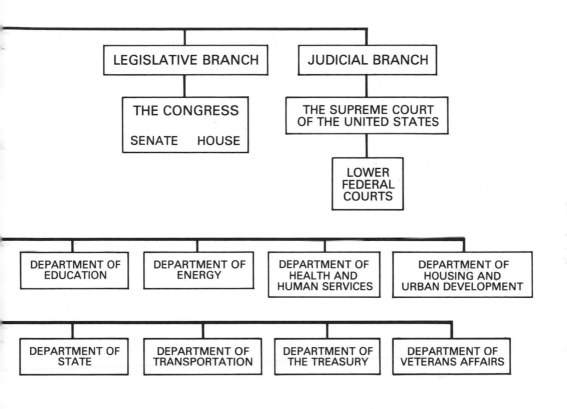

LEGISLATIVE BRANCH

JUDICIAL BRANCH

THE CONGRESS

SENATE    HOUSE

THE SUPREME COURT
OF THE UNITED STATES

LOWER
FEDERAL
COURTS

DEPARTMENT OF
EDUCATION

DEPARTMENT OF
ENERGY

DEPARTMENT OF
HEALTH AND
HUMAN SERVICES

DEPARTMENT OF
HOUSING AND
URBAN DEVELOPMENT

DEPARTMENT OF
STATE

DEPARTMENT OF
TRANSPORTATION

DEPARTMENT OF
THE TREASURY

DEPARTMENT OF
VETERANS AFFAIRS

# GLOSSARY

**Bill**   A piece of proposed legislation introduced into one of the two houses of Congress.

**Cabinet**   An informal advisory body—consisting of the vice-president, the heads of the 14 departments of the executive branch, and certain other senior officials—selected by the president to assist him in making decisions.

**Calendar**   A list of the bills that are eligible for consideration on the floor of either house of Congress.

**Checks and balances**   A system in which the power of each branch of government is controlled or limited by the other branches.

**Elastic clause**   Article I, Section 8 of the Constitution, which gives Congress the power to make whatever laws it decides are necessary.

**Elite theory**   The idea that important political decisions in the United States are made by a small, exclusive group of top-level corporate, military, and political leaders.

**Federal system**   A system of government in which power is divided between the national government and various subnational governments such as states.

**Filibuster**   A marathon speech used by senators to tie up the Senate and prevent a particular bill from being voted on.

**Impeachment**   The process by which a president or other federal officials may be removed from office for having committed, according to the Constitution, "Treason, Bribery or other high Crimes and Misdemeanors."

**Implied powers**   Powers not spelled out by the Constitution but that nevertheless may be exercised by the government.

**Interest group**   An organization of people who have joined together in the attempt to influence policymakers to respond to their needs and concerns.

**Judicial activism**   The view that the Supreme Court should make policy on its own in order to promote desirable social goals.

**Judicial restraint**   The view that the Supreme Court should not initiate policy but instead defer to the legislative and executive branches.

**Judicial review**   The Supreme Court's power to declare unconstitutional the laws or actions of federal or state executives.

**Lobbying**   The process by which representatives of interest groups attempt to influence government policy by communicating directly with policymakers.

**Pluralism**   The concept that democracy is achieved in the United States because many interests have access to the government and compete with each other to influence policy decisions.

**Political action committees (PACs)**   Committees created by interest groups to further their policy goals by channeling money to elect or defeat candidates for political office.

**Quorum**   The minimum number of members who must be present for either the House of Representatives or the Senate to conduct legislative business. The House requires 218 members to be present; the Senate requires 51.

**Rule**   An action, taken by the House Committee on Rules, that determines the amount of time a particular bill can be debated and whether it may be amended.

**Spoils system**   The practice by which victorious politicians reward followers with government jobs.

**Standing committees**   Permanent committees, of the Senate and House of Representatives, that consider bills and conduct hearings on specific legislative matters.

**Supremacy clause**   Article VI, Paragraph 2 of the Constitution, which states that whenever there is a conflict between state and federal law, federal law must prevail.

**Writ of certiorari**   A Supreme Court order in which the Court agrees to hear a case.

# SELECTED REFERENCES

Beard, Charles A. *An Economic Interpretation of the Constitution of the United States.* New York: Macmillan, 1935.

Cummings, Milton C., Jr., and David Wise. *Democracy Under Pressure: An Introduction to the American Political System.* 6th ed. San Diego: Harcourt Brace Jovanovich, 1989.

Dahl, Robert A. *Who Governs?* New Haven, CT: Yale University Press, 1961.

Fenno, Richard F., Jr. *Congressmen in Committees.* Boston: Little, Brown, 1973.

Hughes, Emmet John. *The Living Presidency.* New York: Penguin Books, 1974.

Lowi, Theodore J. *The End of Liberalism: Ideology, Policy, and the Crisis of Public Authority.* 2nd ed. New York: Norton, 1979.

Meltzer, Milton. *American Politics: How It Really Works.* New York: Morrow, 1989.

Mills, C. Wright. *The Power Elite.* New York: Oxford University Press, 1959.

Polsby, Nelson W. *Congress and the Presidency.* 3rd ed. Englewood Cliffs, NJ: Prentice-Hall, 1976.

Riker, William H. *Federalism: Origin, Operation, Significance.* Boston: Little, Brown, 1964.

Rossiter, Clinton. *1787: The Grand Convention.* New York: Macmillan, 1966.

Rourke, Francis E. *Bureaucracy, Politics, and Public Policy.* 3rd ed. Boston: Little, Brown, 1984.

Schlesinger, Arthur M., jr. *The Imperial Presidency.* Boston: Houghton Mifflin, 1973.

Schubert, Glendon. *Judicial Policy-making.* 2nd ed. Glenview, IL: Scott, Foresman, 1974.

Wittenberg, Ernest, and Elisabeth Wittenberg. *How to Win in Washington: Very Practical Advice About Lobbying, the Grassroots, and the Media.* New York: Basil Blackwell, 1989.

# INDEX

139

## PICTURE CREDITS

**Bernotas** is a free-lance writer and editor. He holds a Ph.D. in political ...ory from The Johns Hopkins University and has taught philosophy and ...litical science at Morgan State and Towson State Universities. His published works include a study guide for a textbook on American government and numerous articles on jazz and sports. He lives in Baltimore, Maryland.

**Arthur M. Schlesinger, jr.,** served in the White House as special assistant to Presidents Kennedy and Johnson. He is the author of numerous acclaimed works in American history and has twice been awarded the Pulitzer Prize. He taught history at Harvard College for many years and is currently Albert Schweitzer Professor of the Humanities at the City College of New York.